0100448
237775

THE LIBRARY
CITY COLLEGE PLYMOUTH

My Wheelchair View

By Janice Hobbs Towns

authorHOUSE®

AuthorHouse™
1663 Liberty Drive
Bloomington, IN 47403
www.authorhouse.com
Phone: 1-800-839-8640

© 2012 Janice Hobbs Towns. All rights reserved.

No part of this book may be reproduced, stored in a retrieval system, or transmitted by any means without the written permission of the author.

First published by AuthorHouse 02/28/2012

ISBN: 978-1-4634-1103-9 (sc)
ISBN: 978-1-4634-1105-3 (hc)
ISBN: 978-1-4634-1104-6 (ebk)

Library of Congress Control Number: 2011908853

Printed in the United States of America

Any people depicted in stock imagery provided by Thinkstock are models, and such images are being used for illustrative purposes only. Certain stock imagery © Thinkstock.

This book is printed on acid-free paper.

Because of the dynamic nature of the Internet, any web addresses or links contained in this book may have changed since publication and may no longer be valid. The views expressed in this work are solely those of the author and do not necessarily reflect the views of the publisher, and the publisher hereby disclaims any responsibility for them.

This book is dedicated to my mother Amanda, husband Larry Sr and our children Matese, and John and Larry Jr. Who says I am the record keeper for the family. They enjoyed the stories over and over again.

All of these stories are true. Some of the events may be as I remember. Names could be change to protect the innocent but who cares, I am in a wheelchair. I love my family, and always did the best I could for them.

I feel my family is a colorful union that has different experience and wanted to share them with the world.

Willie Hobbs Sr. (April 6, 2006) my father

Molly Dillard was married to Gave Dillard. She already had a daughter name Catherine whose birthday March 10, 1884 or 1885, was an only child.

Nolen Hobbs was 16 in 1885 the year born 1869.
Elizabeth Hobbs was 5 when the war started. Got married and had 16 children 13 grew to be adults. 3sister Della McCoy (104) never married. Ellis   Lawson

1. Johnnie (South Carolina)
2. Frances (Ind.)
3. Mary (O children, married Hatcher)
4. Bertha (0 children, married Benny Berry-Tunkie
5. Cleveland (Chicago, Ill)
6. Henry (5 children) Molly, Ethel, Willie Sr., Frances and Henry
7. Walter (James)
8. Jesse (week end alco)
9. Nolen (preacher with a lot of childern)
10. Ollie (Frank, Claudia)
11. Bessie (8 children) live to be 107
12. Eddie (1 girl)
13. Lue Lee (3 children)

STORY ABOUT THE FAMILY

Catherine's stepfather was a man that wanted a woman that had another man's interest. The two men were at odds. Grandpapa Gave went to a voodoo woman and said "I just need something to knock the man down then, I know I can beat him". The voodoo woman gave him a stick and said "knock him down with this". When grandpapa Gave had a chance he picked up the stick swung and missed. The man picked up the stick and hit him in the eye. Now he wears an eye patch.

Grand pa Henry

On a nice cool fall day Catherine, Grand pa's wife passes by the church and saw some people cleaning the grave yards. When she got to the house she said" Henry they are working on cleaning the grave yard today. Why don't you go clean off your father's grave"? Henry said back to her while headed for the door "If my father can help me plow and plant this field then I will go and clean off his grave".

My families were always close or lived close by.
Grand papa Henry's sisters lived down the street from my mother's mother. His sister Aunt Mary was very kind. Aunt Ollie was a little different. She was a retired teacher. When Aunt Mary died Aunt Ollie told her sister Bessie, "You come in this house with me or I will come and live with you." Aunt Bessie moved in with Ollie's house because it was bigger. Aunt Ollie did not care for a lot of children. Aunt Betty had 8 children and more than 30 grandchildren. When Aunt Ollie died, we went back to the house for the repast and I heard her daughter say "Well that bitch is dead," And gave Bessie 60 days to move out.

A lady called me and said she was a cousin of mine name McMillan on the Hobbs side of the family. I told her I don't know but I have an Aunt Bessie 105 years old maybe she can tell you. The lady came over to my house and I carried her to Orrville, Alabama to see Bessie Hobbs Edwards. Aunt Bessie is Grandpapa Henry's sister that allowed the family to call her Betty, every one else address her as Bessie. We went in and I let the lady ask question? She said I am McMillan my father lived in Mobile. Are kin to each other? My Aunt said, "I had a cousin named Sally. Sally married a McMillan they had 3 children. The children are names are and she named them. My cousin Sally got sick and died.
McMillan was so upset after her death, he moved to Mobile and married someone else I don't know her. The lady said he married my mother that makes us kin. My aunt looked at me and said the story again. I had a cousin name Sally. She married a man name McMillan. They had 3 children. My cousin Sally got sick and died. The husband McMillan moved to Mobile and married some else "I don't know her (whom he married)." The lady did not tell us what happen to the three older children who are in the Hobbs family
I said Aunt Betty can you tell me any thing else. She talked about an aunt name Ellis her mother's sister. Ellis had a son name Ben. Ben had a son,
Name Little Ben. Little Ben went to a lady house and beat her in front of her husband. The husband shot him in his foot. I said, Aunt Bessie stop shaking that family tree, now its time to go.

I visit aunt Bessie in the Warren Manor Home, for her 107 birthday. She had gotten hard of hearing and didn't see to well. The nurse said your niece Janice is here to see you. She said Janice has a lot of nerves (burn badly and survived). I was proud she remember me.
Aunt Bessie's daughter died. The family members choose not to tell her, which I though was a mistake. Her son came to visit her and she said "Amos do you know why my daughter Lillian has not been by to see me". Her son Amos said" because I killed her." She was so upset. The family had to come and tell her the truth. It was not long after that aunt Bessie died.

Earleen was home when Grandpa Henry came over complaining about a headache. He said "My head hurt so bad, what can you give me something to help" Earleen looked around but could not find anything like an aspirin, or goody. She took a pill and gave him some water. He took it quickly. To her surprise he announces he felt better. She was amazed. When he said "I got to go. But before I go will you give me another pill in case my headache comes back." She returned from the kitchen with another pill and told him that it is a powerful pill and that the s on the pill stands for super. After he left she had to laugh because the s really stands for sugar.

Aunt Ethel had two daughters Earleen and Jean Smith. When the girls were young, she sent them over to a neighbor's house for a visit. The girl's mother was surprised but let them in. When Jean and Earleen got ready to go home and said "Here is an extra hug from our mother". A week later they were sick with chicken pots. Jean said "I don't understand why or how this happen." Her mother said, "that's the reason I sent you over to the neighbor's house with an extra hug from me. I wanted you get chicken pots out the way so you would not miss any school".

We were visiting Aunt Ethel, She made us lunch that day. My husband and cousin Sandra was nine years old. On the way home Sandra asked me a question that made my heart stop. She asked me what happen to the lady that live upstairs why didn't she come down for lunch. I said "WHAT LADY!" Sandra said "When I asked to use the bathroom"; Aunt Ethel said "use the one upstairs". Sandra said, "I saw a lady at the top of the stairs. She didn't say anything. After the bathroom I didn't see her anymore". I said "what did she look like"? She describes my grandmother Catherine to a T, whom died when I was nine years old.

Aunt Ethel took on the job to raise her granddaughter. Her daughter Earleen died in a car accident in 1972 in Lancaster, Penn. Aunt Ethel dressed the girl out of the Salvation Army or the Thrift shop. I met up with Sharon in the Montgomery Eastdale Mall one day close to Christmas. I told Sharon, (age 14) that I wanted to give her a present for Christmas. We went to Parisian's and found an outfit on sale. I told her that her grandmother will not like it. I want you to open it on Christmas day when I am not around. You know what is in the box because you have tried everything on. The top and jeans fitted accordingly to her age. Sharon waited and decided to act surprised as planned. Aunt Ethel made Sharon return it to get a bigger size or something else. When they got to the store because it was on sale they didn't have any thing else and she end up with what she had in the first which made Sharon happy.

Aunt Ethel received money from Earleen's death. She got $80,000 double indemnity insurance for the accidental death of her daughter in Lancaster, Penn. She gave her daughter Jean 20,000 for her children but took it back after a month. She gave other gifts to family members but cheap gifts to the two people who was in the car with her daughter. Aunt Ethel got colon cancer. Aunt Ethel made sure she had control and again selected helped the two that was in the car with her daughter. I was in the room with Aunt Ethel when she died. Her daughter Jean and my husband also were in the room. We were talking when Jean notice the difference in her mother's breathe. We called the nurse and the nurse pronounced her dead. While we were waiting for the coroner to come, I left to pick up my children and head the 50 miles home. When I got home my dad called to tell me Aunt died. I said I know, because I was there.

Aunt Ethel went to her dad's sister Bessie house. The doctor and family decided that the 105 year old was better off in a nursing home. Aunt Ethel was supposed to take some clothes to the home on Aunt Bessie behalf.
Although Aunt Bessie daughter lived next door was busy but told

Aunt Ethel she will come and help when she finished what she was doing. When Aunt Ethel got into the house she took pictures off the wall and what ever else she wanted and left. Aunt Ethel got copies of the pictures and sold them for $10 each. The pictures were of Aunt Bessie parents, one of her mother Elizabeth and one of her father Nolen. Aunt Bessie children did not like it but what could you do.

Grand pa Henry's mother Elizabeth says she only raised teachers and preachers. But most people say they were drunks and skunks. Willie Hobbs Sr. talks as if his father did everything to make their life difficult. Henry own land that he sold for very little because he did not want his children to have it.

My cousin Jean married a military man. Which required them to move around and be station all over the United States? My cousin had her babies in the state of Alabama because she felt it will be easy for her girls to get information in one spot instead of all over the world because her husband was in the Air Force service. They have been station from San Antonia, Texas to Alaska. After she had the baby her husband asked one question? What the sex or weight or what....... no but the color of his baby's eyes.

Jean's family had a water gun day. On Saturday they would spray each other got close to one another they would give a little squeak. They sneak up on each other and had a different color guns. Jean had 2 or 3 hidden and when they least suspect it, she give them a bath. They sometime double up on each other.

My family went to Las Vegas for a vacation. We were over visiting at my Cousin Jean's house when she pick up the telephone and made a call. She made five calls trying to locate her daughter Rhonda. Each time she talks to daughter's roommate, asking her to leave a note on Rhonda's door that says 'her mother call and going to kill her". Rhonda came over and explained she had gone to get a manicure and pedicure.

I said how many times your mother said she is going to kill you to you. She said "everyday of my life except once when she got laryngitis then she wrote it on a piece of paper.

In Las Vegas, my cousin decided to punish my daughter Matese who was 3 years old. Jean places her in a bedroom for 5 minutes. She asked me if I mind. I said knock yourself out. Jean went to check on her after the 5 minutes. She came back with Matese in hand she said "Do you know what your child was doing?" I said," No, what?" She said "Matese was playing with a paper piñata that was hanging on the wall way up high". I said," well did I tell you that she climbs walls, you can't punish her by putting her in a room because she likes being by herself. Now how would you like to punish her?"

Stephanie went to pre-medical school looking forward to the year. The professor talk for a while and then had the dead bodies rolled in, and the doctor said get to know them. They have been donated by caring human who wants medicine to be a success in the further. Stephanie rolled up out of class and study Law.

Jean's daughter Stephanie is a lawyer. She decided to go on an adventure walk because she stays in an office most of the time. She took a five mile walk on a Saturday. Her neighbor has a dog, so Stephaine asked if she could take her dog with her to have some company. The neighbor said yes that will give him some exercise. After the instruction the group got their backpack with water and started walking. The dog seemed happy, but after a few miles he turned to look at Stephaine as if to say How far? The last mile she picked him up and carried him to the car. Now when she visits the neighbor the dog hides.

Grandpa Henry had one favorite grandchild Willie Jr. name after his son Willie sr. We went for a visit my sister 17 years old and 20 years old brother. He said "it is good to see you grand children but before you leave I have something to give you grandson. We were about to leave when Willie said "Grandpa what is it you want to give me."

He pulls out a box and gave it to him. My brother said "Thank you grandpa". I was 14 asked my brother what's in the box? He said "6-marbles, red ball, football, a spinning top, and two big marbles. My sister and I said at the same time "What are you going to do with that stuff. Willie said, "Well, I guess it make him feel good to give these things for me". I said shouldn't someone tell him that you are in your 2nd year of college.

Grandpapa Henry and Grandmother Catherine had been divorce for a long time. My mother said that he came to live with his son and his family. He dated a woman on several streets down from the house. He would get on the telephone, talking saying "if I come by will you do (then repeat what he heard) you won't do". "I will come up Bone and down Jackson will you do. You won't do, you won't do".

Aunt Fran invited her niece to stay the night. She loves her dog. A rottweiler and she can tell you his weight, head size in inches, how long (head to tail) and how smart he is and what he eats. She talks and every other sentence is about her dog. Well the niece spent the night. She got up to go to the bathroom, but what about the dog? She called and called for some one to put the dog outside so she could go to the bathroom. She couldn't get anyone. So she looked the room up and down to find something big enough to put pee in. Found nothing she went back to calling and finally her first cousin, Aunt Fran's son heard her and put the dog out. The next day the niece went to a hotel.

We went to a farm in the Hobbs family in Orrville, Alabama. We ended up staying for dinner. The hostess prepared a lovely meal. We sat at the table and said grace then we began to eat the food. My brother asked for seconds. The hostess said that is strange most people don't like goat. WE children began to cough and for the next week we teased each other with n-o-o and n-a-y. Every since that day I ask before I eat what kind of meat is this.

Cousin Claudia was visiting me. She asked how I was coping with being a mother with two young children. I am fine. Matese was put out to school at 2. I told her she could not have any of her Birthday cake so early in the morning. She climbed up on a table to the refrigerator and got it. So I carried her to Mcrae's school setting for young children. The bus driver said I may have a problem finding your house in the morning. I told her I am leaving Matese and you will bring her home this evening. You will not have a problem in the morning.

It was hard for me to potty train our son. Don't buy pull-up. I put him in training pants and when he soiled them I made him wash. She said what? I make him wash because he needed to know both how to get mess and how to get clean. It did not take long before he was train. Cousin Claudia went home to Philly and was on the phone with her granddaughter (4 years old) talking. Her daughter lives in Baltimore,

remind her daughter that they had to go to the store. Cousin Claudia said for what. The granddaughter said pull-up.
Cousin Claudia said "PUT YOUR MOTHER ON THE PHONE" She told her what I did in little old Selma. Claudia's daughter got some training pants put them on her daughter explain that when they become soil then she will wash. Her daughter said what you mean put my hand in what.
The girl was train within a month.

A man cooked in a big pot out in his front yard (soup or stews) would invited the neighbors children to eat with him. My mom said she hated to see her children over there because this man had the children jump up and down every time they take a bite. He tells them jumping makes it go down better. She cooks good meals, then looked out the window and saw them (children) jumping. He would laugh.

I loved Grandpa Henry, he was a man that loved women and alcohol drinks. On one of our visits my dad asked his dad where he was hiding his bottle. He said "I don't have one". My dad went into his kitchen and started opening cabinet's doors and refrigerator, my Grandpa Henry never took his eyes off his son from his chair in the living room that was positioned just in the middle of his little apartment. Then my dad got a little to close to something because my grandpa got up and told his son to get out. I was by the door and ready to go. On our way home my dad's car broke down on the highway. My dad and sister and I were standing on the highway trying to get help to fix his car or a ride back to Selma. A truck pulled up and said get in I am going that way. The trucker was a *black* one armed man. This is in the day when the Fugitive was a TV weekly show. No one told me that it was a *white* one armed man so I was scared out of my mind. My dad said "Get in". I said "Where" He lifted us into the cab of that truck and the man carried us to Selma on the other side of town. He left us on the street and called our mother to pick us up. That was the day I will never forget because I made up in my mind that I would not go *anywhere* with my dad again.

A cousin was planning her wedding. She had just gotten her invitation in mail. The guy (groom) showed up at her house and handed her an envelope. She opened it. It was an invitation to a wedding. Wedding with the guy named as the groom and the date was just ahead of the date she had put on the invitation to marry him. He did not have the heart to tell her.

At the family gathering every one was admiring a baby. Saying that baby is so…..and it looks just like…… need to………… The next year the mother had another baby. Then you would think everything was fine. Those same ladies say it to light skin to be his baby and then said the same thing again. The mother told those old birds it no pleasing them.

I called Jean and asked how are things, what about her class this year. Jean said I just met the class from Hell. Half are boys and half are girls most are from broken homes. Their parents are on drugs or they lived in extended family home (grandmother or aunt). I have to punish one or two each day. "How do you do that?" I asked. She said "When we have pizza party the one's that have not done their work put their head on their desk. Let the others eat and have fun."
I told them that" if I pass out due to my diabetes go get the teacher from next door. She will know what to do."
This one boy said "I will save you I will give you mouth to mouth". Jean said "No, you guys (are in the 4th grade) just go get the teacher from next door." "I can resuscitate you I love to help" said the excited boy. Jean said "Look if I wake up and catch your on my lips on mine I will knock you out, as soon as I can get up. I don't want you anywhere near my lips."

Jean is a retired teacher who ran across one of her former student in the mall. The boy had his brother and one other friend with him. The student said we are going to see a movie that is PG17 but my little brother has to have an adult to buy his ticket will you get it for us, it will only take 10 minutes at the most. When they reach the movie the lines were very long. The little brother looked at Jean and said you are a senior citizen and will get a discount why can't we go to the front of the line? They should let you get in the front of the line. Jean smiled and though (what kind of discount will I get in jail if something happen to him).

Jean wants a divorce from her husband after 25 years of marriage. Their divorce will be final when he pays her money that covered the interest she put in the house. She told him her mother was divorced and her grandmother was also divorced, and he was on borrow time. Her mother Ethel had colon cancer. So Jean started taken her health serious.
She had to go to the out clinic to have a procedure done and need someone to pick her up. Her ex husband said he will do it. After Jean

had seen the doctor who said "you could go home" and asked "who is here with you? I will go and get him." When the ex walked back, and opened the curtain Jean was just stepping into her red panties. The next visit when the doctor said she had to have more test done. She said since my ex-husband has seen my red panties. I better wear the green ones next time.

Janice Hobbs Towns

My hair dresser told me this story in her shop.
In the early 70's she had 6 children. The pill was just coming out and when she had her check up she asked the doctor for them. Her husband said "no wife of his will ever take birth control pills". I ask her "what did you do"? She said she told him "He can go to work and I will take them. Or you can stay here and watch me because I will take them like a chicken swallowing corn."

In that same shop I talked with Barbara who was a costumer, said she did not like her 16 years old son talking on the telephone. I told her she has two choices 1) get another phone so he can talk to his friends, and be happy you know where he is or 2) denied him the phone and let him *go out* to see his friends. Before you answer remember teen boys don't all ways do what is expected of them. She said well I guess I will get another telephone.

Willie Hobbs (dad)

I know you can't pick your parents.
When I was small I felt I had a part time father, a person that give only a fraction of one self to his family, church, job. He was always gone. I can't remember seeing him in church, at our school, talking about his job, or playing a simple game. The only place was the kitchen table to eat.
He taught me how not to be. I learn to be fair, kind, loving, caring, and polite. When at one time you are doing these things you are (not) a good person. He was always thinking between some woman legs. Then when he ran out of places, he went to church and got women there. His children were never at the top of his list, he never had a list. Now he comes to see me at my house. And had the nerve to fuss when I was not home, I told him "I am the only one of his children that NEVER looked for him". I joy ride with my sister or brother to get out of the house.

One day my brothers were doing some much needed work around the hot water heater. Little Willie and Cleophus worked all day. Willie Sr. came home after who knows what and said they did it wrong. Pressing the fact and pushed one of the boys. A fight broke out Willie sr. called the police and refuse to get them out of jail. Hen told my mother that they disrespected him. And she told him" You better get them Now or else". He got them out by dropping the charges. I raised my sons and not one had been in and out of jail for none sense.

After my accident may mother stayed with my father for 3 years.

When expense money came up he wanted to be paid back everything he ever got for us. On the list were books, gown, trips to see me, TV. And happy meals

The expense money turned to be part of the settlement he wanted from my mother. He said "when I left the first time, I carried nothing but this time I want more." It was only 10,000. He wanted half and another 3,000 for building 3 rooms added to the house. A place he laid his head. After seeing the lawyer one day my mother says what to do". I said "give it to him." So he got eight thousand a 25 inches TV and a big heater. The items, somehow found its way to baby mama's house. My mom got 2 thousand. In the years that follow my mother and father became the best of friends.

Willie Sr. was a whore hopping son of gun that loved women. He was at our house for a visit when a woman weighed 300 lbs was trying to cut his tires because he was dating her. She did not know why he was at our house but she knew he was not where he was supposed to be. My sister saw her and said "dad someone is around your car'. He ran out and the lady started running him around with a butcher knife they must have run around that car 3 times. My sister and I laughed and laughed. I said "dad do you want me to get the gun." He said "YES, GET THE GUN". That lady took off down the street running for her life. And NO, we did not have a gun, but she did not know that.

Our father married 5 times twice to our mother, and lived with whoever would take him in. Willie Jr. wanted to get some money from his father to buy a tool. We went over to his new (second) wife of two months house. Ms. Annie Mae was a muscle woman that seen to know how to treat him. We found him in the dark cutting grass with a lawn-mower with flash light attach to the handle. He would fight women and this one fought back.

My mother remarried my dad after a 10 year split. A lady came over to our house for a visit. My mom said, "I've got to go to work in the morning, so I better say good night." I looked at my mom with one question in mind. Who is this and when is she leaving? I was not about to go to bed with a stranger in the house. Mom said she was her classmate's sister. After mom went to bed, that lady started talking 5 miles a minute. She talked about how Willie cut her grass and laid down in her bed. Then she looked at me and said I mean you brother, Willie Jr. I said you might mean my father Willie Sr., because my brother Willie Jr. would not lie in your bed. On the other hand …….Willie Sr. walked in the door. She said "Hobbs, where have you been? I looked at him and said "Yes, *Hobbs*, where have you been?" He took her home.

Willie Sr. married to his fourth wife. He would say how he preached on Sunday and had her running in her panties all week. They were married for 13 years. He was telling his two grown daughters when one daughter Gladys, from out of town said, "That woman (his wife) is a Saint, She stays with you live in *her* house and she gives you all *her* money and you still have *her* running". It is clear that woman is a saint.

I can't tell you how many children my father has because he never admitted to any more than 12 (included 8 of his wife's). But a cousin once told me he had 17 before he married his last wife. He introduced one on the graveyard to his sister Ethel. I said "now isn't that tacky".

Willie Hobbs Sr. Stayed married to my mom for a number of years because he told her with her money and his brains we can make it. The only reason they divorce was because he took money out of their joint account to pay for his child born to another woman. The money belongs to the school coco cola machine. She had to borrow the money to pay it back. After the divorce, he refused to pay child support.

Everyone thinks Dianne is like her father. We were at church for his anniversary. He talked most about Dianne who choose not to come. On father's day, he calls us and say" we are out of his will". He wants us to visit him at his house or go fishing. He is in his eighty's now he wants to be a father.

After my father divorce his fourth wife he wanted to get back with my mother. He asked her sister Florence to help. Florence started telling mother how Willie is doing saying and feeling. Florence told me to stay out of it. I told her she is single and can marry him her self. It is a different day.

My father was in between wives when he met Ms. Green and had a son. He moved on to another woman, so Ms. Green wanted him to pay child support. My father went to court and told the judge. He was too old to make a baby. A friend called and told me she saw my father in court. I asked dad about it. He said Yes, I told that judge I was old. I said "I bet the boy look just like you". He said" Yes, he sure does".

Ms. Green died and her son came looking for his next of kin. The home house had Dianne and her family. They moved back from Milwaukee, Wisconsin. Dianne told the boy to come in because she was sure her brother didn't know he had a son. She asked him what is his mother's name, I don't know her but I lived away in Milwaukee. Well, she said "I will call Janice to see if Willie Jr. had a son? Janice (on the phone) this young man is here and he said his mother name is Ms. Green and how come you didn't tell me Willie Jr. have a son? I said you know our brother's are not like our father. Just don't believe that our brothers would have children not let us know.
"Dianne you were in Milwaukee (10 years) when this happen, look at the boy good because that boy is not your nephew but He is your brother, Willie Sr.'s son". Dianne got mad and told him to get out.

On our side of Minter, there were families that lived their whole lives in one house. Mr. and Mrs. Lawson was and old couple. Mrs. Collins a widow.
There was a family of 3 older boys with their father because their mother died. Mr. and Mrs. Reed and next to them Mr. and Mrs.

Barlow and our house and on the corner Mr. and Mrs. Williams, we were neighbors for six years.

On the other side renters stayed for 1 years or longer. Getting to know the neighbors was easy because everybody know everybody. FEFE Lawson was a gay man that lived with his grandparents, on the corner house; it was a story going around town about a girl getting beat up on her street in front of her house. Her sister was home did nothing but she could see everything. He was upset and said "Janice, you know that would not do, if someone comes into this neighborhood and hitting on your sister, and no one help or say nothing. That just would not happen here on Minter". I look at him and said "FEFE, you mean *my* sister? Well if my sister was getting beat up on this block, NO, I would not help her because if she can not beat one person, it makes No sense for me to get beat too. I see no point for two of us to get our ass kick. He walked off fast, with out saying a word.

Mrs. Reed was a school teacher, and she died. Mr. Reed dated a married woman at our church. The church member's husband came over to our house and asked if my mother had seen his wife over to Mr. Reed's house. It was only two doors from our house. My mom said "Yes, we see your wife and all the other neighbors see her too".

At our church a lady was told her son had a baby by a girl in our community. The lady had 6 sons and all had or were having babies to which she would respond "My sons not the only ones with penis (dicks)".

Across the street was a lady with a lot of children all ages. The teen girl had a lot of friends. One was a gay boy named Junior (high pitch voice) his mother (low pitch voice) would come looking for him if he did show up on time at home. Junior's Mother calls for him to come out the house. It sound like: Junior come out that house *I ain't coming mama, I ain't coming* . Junior I am tired from work come on now the he answer *I ain't coming mama I ain't coming*. After going around 3 or 4 times the neighbors got involved. Mister Barlow would say" If

you all don't stop I will call the police!" Then the mother would tell Mister Barlow off. "I know you. Mister Barlow the painter and you can't paint that good."
After 2 hours of going back and forth, until Junior's mama pleaded for Mister Barlow to help her. Mister Barlow can you (please) come and help me get my son.
We would just sit at the window and laugh, not much television in those days.

Mister Barlow didn't like children, having five next door was the last straw.
He went as far as getting a petition and wanted the neighbors to sign.
He tried to do or say something to let us know we were not welcome (every day he got a chance). With my brother Nolen: Nolen and his friends would hit golf balls in our yard. When you play ball don't hit it to his yard he would keep the ball.
He said something and Nolen told him Mister Barlow if you don't stop I will have my friends put your flowers in the middle of Broad Street (busy street). Mister Barlow loved his flowers he water them sometimes more than twice a day. He left Nolen alone.
With my brother Willie he complained he had too many friends. Willie said they are my drinking buddy not yours. He started drinking with them too.
He left Willie alone.
Now, Dianne's turn she had words (cuss-out) with him then Mister Barlow had her to fix his painters pants putting a button on flap and paid her for doing the work. He and Dianne got alone fine after that.
Janice, I was standing on the pouch, and he said little girl I know you don't stay there so go home. I said "I am home. Leave me alone." I guess he did not recognize me since I had a wig on.

Mister Barlow wanted to put up a fence. He wanted to have room to walk around his house. He asked my mother to sell him a foot of land. My mother said NO! He made sure the fence was put up while we were at school and took the foot of land any way. My mother did not make him moved the fence.

Linda Williams lived on the other corner house, next to our house. She always teased us about our not having a good father. On week ends because she went to school in Marengo county. Both our moms were teachers. Mrs. Lela Williams' husband worked on the railroads.
Mom explain to us that our father like to play with a lots of women and not like to stay home. He was living with a lady that lived 7 blocks down the street. She didn't like him playing with so many women so he could not live with us. We understand.
Linda's mother got killed in a car accident in 1970, when she was 16 at the time. Mrs. Williams got hit by a Detroit police offer on a chase. Mrs. Williams died right away and the others got injury. They sued and got some money how much? I don't know.
In just 2 years, Linda went from a loving daughter to calling her dad all kinds of mother fuckers: bald head. Cross eyed cheating etc. up to an hour at a time. One day Linda ran her father with a knife. He got married and left.
We found out she was adopted after her mother died.
A lady in the area where she taught school was having a baby and said I will give you this baby. You are so nice. The reason Linda was so angry, she though her adopted dad would send her home to her birth parents.

Mr. and Mrs. Depass was an old couple on a corner from us. The man threw paper across the street. He would walk around his yard and find pieces of paper. He picks it up walks to the end of his yard and tosses it across the street. His wife stayed at the house most of the time had very few friends. When she died she had one family car and one car to follow. Her husband, one friend, and 2 neighbors, all could fit in one car. Mrs. Depass's last will, says she gave the house to her Catholic Church. The house contents to the Heart Association. The one friend's son bought the furniture gave the money to the Heart

Association.. Her husband got a bed a dresser and chair. He could live in the house until he died or until the church ask him to move.

My mother got hit by a car that sent her into Mr. Depass' fence. He comes to our door every day to ask when she will get the fence fixed. He brought a piece of paper for her to signed, to get the fence fixed. Mother said my insurance company told me to tell you it is the other car's fault and not to sign anything. The other driver was their church member driving her boyfriend's car. The boyfriend had to fix the fence and my mom's car.

Linda plays the piano and I wanted her to play for my wedding. When I told her I will be getting married on the 18 of December. She said I thought I would be married before you (handicapped in a wheeled chair).
I said you have up to the 17th of December. Now can you play for my wedding? She said "Yes" I married before she did, it was in Jet magazine (Jan 83).

My sister and I were sitting on the porch when a man was walking down the street. Two boys were at the corner up to mischief said Raymond, Raymond who shot the mule? Raymond was a tall slim man you can say a black Abe Lincoln. We ran into the house and got by the window to see what would happen next. It was said he picks up rocks and throw them at whomever playing prank on him. The boys repeated Raymond, Raymond who shot that mule. He walks not breaking a stride he said "your goddamn mama shot that goddamn mule."

On the corner house across the street was a family. Mother, father and children, the mother was a home maker because she had 6 children. The husband worked all week and on Friday he had his time. He would spend the week walking and talking with the neighbors. Friday evening to Sunday morning he was drunk. Not sleep drunk, but wobble down the street drunk. He could not get up the seven steps to get into his house. The children would call for mommy to help. His wife would come out side take off her shoe and whip him up the steps. The father's mother lived down the street from her son, did the same thing. The father's mother kept children all week. Come pay day she was with her son sloppy drunk. The two of them walking down the street was a sight to see. One time she was trying to hold him up. They would sober up to go to church on Sunday.

My 9th grade science teacher Ms. Law told us about her brother. He walks to see his girlfriend a date evening that go into night. On the way home he goes by a cemetery walking home he heard someone say, where have you been? He told whoever the answer. The questions kept on coming? How far is that? And who is that? By that time they had made it to the corner of the street. Then it said I can't go across the street. He looked to see who he was talking to and found nothing. He ran all the way home. From that day forward, he did every thing in the day time hours. He dated and married during the day light.

We were at school when Mr. Jones my lunch teacher was walking to the cafeteria with a cane. He and Ms. Law talking and he saying Author and Rudy got him this morning. A student said Mr. Jones you should be ashamed of yourself going with another woman and her husband has to beat you up. He said no fool, arthritis and rheumatism boy. The whole cafeteria laughed.

Mrs. Law was a science teacher. She believed in given children something they can use. So our science class went to see how oil is change. Dissect frogs, until a student name Rosemary with blond hair cried. I would get the frogs because my mother students caught them for me from the country. We did a lot of chemical experiments. She would tell us short stories that made sense.

MY SISTER

Dianne at age 16 carried me to go and find Willie Hobbs Sr. She wanted some money to buy herself a blouse. We found him working on a car down the street from the woman he was staying with. Dianne said "Daddy I need some money for this blouse"? He said, "Go to the house and tell Mozell to give you 15 dollars". Willie, Dianne, Janice three children 15 dollars which means 5 dollars per child. When Dianne got to the door she said Daddy want us to have 20 dollars. Then she hit at me at the door because she knew I would correct her. I went back to the car. Then she bought her blouse. A couple of days later Daddy told her not to do it again.

Dianne's son Togo tells his sister Stephanie that she is an accident. The daughter calls him a mistake. They have conversation on who will get mom when she get old No one wins.

I came home from shopping and found my sister in my house. I asked how she got in, and she said someone gave her a key. I put my hand out and said "That somebody lied. She put the key in my hand. I took it".

Grand mother Lucy had a broken hip, When Dianne made a visit to help. Auntie Violet wanted to put the something in the garage in the trash. Violet's daughter lived up stairs with her husband. When Dianne put the garage in the trash the husband called the police. The police let her out on her own bond. AT the hearing the judge listen two both sides. The husband went first. Dianne told the judge that

My Wheelchair View

her cousin's husband wanted to go with her and that this is a mess because him. Judge says Family Matter Dismiss.

My sister is 3 years older than me. She has always like things her way. If it is not her way then you are wrong just wrong. When we were small she ran the house, even if it was in her mind only. Mother would go to the store, she find me to tell me something to do. I did it. One day I asked my mom why Dianne was so mean. She told me I was her daughter and Dianne was my sister. From that day forward when she say mother gone now get this done. I left out the door and head to grandma house. When she checks to see if the work was done, she found me gone. I came home when my mother return. She would hit me but if I stayed and did the task she hit me.
My sister told me that Willie Hobbs Sr. was not my daddy. She was mad one day and said in the heat of angry that Willie Hobbs ain't your dad. Instead of being sad, I felt happy for a change. I asked my mother "will you tell me who is my daddy because I found out that Willie Hobbs is not. Where did you find that my mother said, I didn't want to say your daughter Dianne. Then she said Willie is the only one I know. …..I said "Damn".

I was ten years old, my mother wanted to give me a surprise party. My sister asked all my friends and our cousins to come I got a surprise because no one showed but you guess it Dianne friends. My mother said "Dianne go to the store and get one handkerchief with laces". Which mean cake with coconut frosting my favorite at that time? Along the way every friend Dianne met she invited to her sister's party. Her friends out number mine.

Dianne gave her 10 year old son a party. The decoration was different color condom. Of course they didn't know what they were. They through the condoms were balloons.

Dianne and Janice had a day of cleaning when a knock was at the door. Maurice came over to drop off something for my mother from his mother. After he left a fly started flying around. Dianne said who let the fly in. I said Maurice. And from then on we call all flies Maurice. When I go to a restaurant and see Maurice we don't eat salad from an open salad bar.

I was with Dianne and her children at a restaurant in Milwaukee. Her daughter got sick and threw up. I said "Let's go home and maybe she will feel better". Then her son got up and ran to the bathroom .She called the waiter over and said clean up on this floor, as she continues her lunch. My children know how to make themselves feel better. I was shock!

A lady's son got in trouble for touching little girls inappropriate. His mother worked in the office of the superintendent. The family had a funeral business. Dianne said may be if he had learn to fuck the dead instead of children then nobody would have complain. The children sued and got undisclosed amount money. He got time in jail.

Picture a 4'10" about 150 pounds bald head and 40DD bust size. We were riding down the street when a police stop us for speeding. The policeman approaches the car saying "Boy! Where are you going so fast?" He turned 3 shades of red, when she got out of the car. He was so nervous he said just slow it down. She had been known to drive a little fast; a cousin asked if she got her license at the 5 and 10 cent store.

We had dances at the local YMCA. A guy asking around for spare change, when he spotted Dianne at the popcorn machine. He asked her what she had in her pocket. He saw her put change it her pocket. She looked at him and said "ME. I have me in my pocket." He looked to her back side and said well you must have a whole in your pocket, because I see some back here too.

I was in a car accident when I was 15. I stayed in the hospital for 9 months at a time. I was in a Birmingham hospital, when in walked

Dianne and Little Willie. My sister Dianne began by saying "Janice, I wish you hurry up and die. I am tried of coming up to visit you. We are suing that trucking company that hit you're car and whatever money we get will be well spent". I looked at my brother Willie and he said nothing. She continued "We are tried of you, so hurry up and kick that bucket. Because we don't need this, I have my dress ready." I was shock and didn't know what to say.

Dianne got mad with mother and told her she didn't want stay to with us anymore. So mama said go and stay with her father. She packed a bag of clothes. Mama said no let me help you pack. My brother had to take her to Orrville, about 15 miles from us. Dianne got to the first stop sign at the end of the block and got out the car and walked home.

We were in the kitchen when my father asked for some butter. My sister didn't want to do it. She went to the refrigerator and got the butter but made a strange trip near the sink then back to my father. Putting the butter in front of him, she didn't say anything. He told her to butter her bread first. Then he said it louder. She took the butter and put it in the trash later she told me that she put devil lye on it.
Dianne was in college. Living in a dorm is a sharing experience. Her roommates had to share with 3 other girl's one bathroom. One day while Dianne was in the bathroom, one girl decided to confronts her and start a fight. One reason is because Dianne was the littlest and the girl felt she can beat her. Dianne put a licking on that girl and she called for help but not before Dianne put a bite on her. Needless to say she never wanted to be left in a room with her again.

Sister Dianne has a daughter Stephanie that calls her mother Satan. She loves to get into you business large or small. She says "You can't hang out with the owls and get up with the chickens.
In junior high school she made a D. Stephanie was whipped. Her mother was call to the High school, because Stephanie was not paying attention and reading a book, after finishing a test. "Let's get this

straight; you called me here to tell me my daughter was called into the office for reading her personal book. What is school for if not to read something?" said her mother. Because of her mother, Stephanie got detention.

Stephanie was 23 when she got pregnant Dianne got mad and told her this was a bad time to have a baby. Carried her to the clinic, the nurse ask her if this is what you want to do. Stephanie said "I want my baby". The lady told her to go home and not to be afraid of her mother. Dianne didn't speak to her for a week.

Satan (Dianne) now has a grand daughter name demon (Jada). Dianne whipped her with a belt. Jada was 2 years old got that belt whipped her back. Dianne told "Jada I won't hit you any more, and you stop hitting too".

Jada colored with crayons in coloring books at grand auntie Janice house. Jada didn't like the picture Janice had colored. She said you can color in my book but don't color the tree that color. Janice explained that coloring is a way of express one self. It Okays, to color something in a different way to express one self. Jada took her book and said not in my book and you are not my auntie any more neither. Jada is 4, and Janice is 50 and said Thank You. Next day Auntie Janice come and color with me? Yes, just in a minute.

Jada (2 years old) was running around the house to see what everyone was doing. When Matese decided to put her in one place and make her stay. She put her in the den, but there is an opening toward the kitchen and Matese heard Jada trying to get out but found she could not get the door to open. The Jada sat in the middle of the room and said "that bitch". Matese found me in my room and said "Mama I am not have you any grand children! "

My daughter was in the hospital. She went to the doctor because of dizziness. He told her go to the hospital just for over night observation and test. This was her first experience ever with blood test and tubes. They had a monitor on her heart, put a in her hand I stayed to be with her because she was nervous. Aunt Dianne called on the telephone and said "I heard you were in the hospital, hope you are a right but if you need a ride to the graveyard I will much abides and gladly take you."

A lady calls from Milwaukee to say I was unfair to my sister and she was crying. I asked her "Who are you". A friend she said. I said, "Okay, since you call me I feel I should let you know what I have done for Dianne. I gave her allowance money for college, paid for her wedding. Help raise her son (10 months to 3 years while she was in college). She and her husband sold a car that was in my name without telling me. I gave her the car she was driving. Help moved them to Milwaukee. I stayed 6 weeks to help with her new baby. And now you want me to send her money to buy who knows what? The lady said now that I know all of that I will leave you alone and I will not call her again.

A lady calls my friend Linda and said "I want to know why you call my house for my husband?" Linda said "No, I did not call your house". The lady continued "yes you did, because I got your number from the caller I D and you call here for my husband" Linda said No but do you have any children around 12 years old. She said yes. Linda said well my children must have called looking for one of your children but as soon as I get off this telephone they won't be calling back.

Stephanie lived with her grandmother, Nancy, her father Edward have one sister name Gwen. Ms. Nancy is a retired teacher and she is having health problems. Stephanie had been helping with the care of her grand mother but her daughter that lived in California wanted to be closer to her mother, moved back to help. Everything was taken over by her daughter. Four generation living together, so Stephanie decided to move out. I told her a little girl does not need 3 mothers. She will be confused as to whom in charge.
The police were called because Stephanie and Gwen were having a disagreement. Gwen (Dad's sister) asked for the keys to the car and the house. Stephanie just graduated from college less than 2 weeks

ago, and worked part time. Her daughter was with her grandmother Dianne. The police said work it out. Stephanie if your aunt and grand mother want you to stay away then does it that way. Stephanie said "but sometimes I call and the ringer is off telephone, or sometimes my grand mama need food or need help to the bathroom. I come by to help." Gwen said "Stephanie, finished college and have moved out so give me the keys now: Stephanie was hurt but gave them up.

Dianne called Gwen and said. Why, did you have the need to call the police on my daughter? All of you have lived in the same house for over 2 years together. I know you needed the car, no two grown ass women need to have just one car.

We made trip to Milwaukee, to my sister house. June, a friend of Dianne's, was going to the local store. Dianne decided to go along with her. Next thing we knew we were getting a call from the police station. "Bail! For what! Yes will I bring the money" her husband said. My brother Willie went with her husband to pick them up. Talking about what happen the two ladies began by saying June got stop by the cops for speeding and running a check on her license turn up parking tickets. Why the officers were talking to her in their car Dianne knocked on the window and said "How long will this take because I have family from Alabama." They asked her name and ran her check on her license and found parking tickets too. They took both down to the station. Dianne looked at June and said "June, I ain't riding with you no more!!!!~!"

My sister had a car tag that reads "To know me is to Love me". She wanted something like BLACK B-i-t-c-h, something she was proud of.
In college her name was Coke, because she wore coke cola hot pants.

Dianne had a friend named Val who was going with an older man. One day Val called Coach (older man) and a woman answer the telephone. Val asked to speak to coach and the lady said He is not here. Val called the bus deport and got the time the bus will be in his town. Then she called back and told the lady she wanted to leave a message for coach. Tell him Val will be on the 8:15 bus in his town. Thank You. When Coach came home and called Val. She assured him she will be on that bus. The time came and was Val ready to go? Val is you going? Val said "No, I'm not going. He will have to send her home. When Coach get ride of the lady he's with and I am not going. He will get no play (sex) tonight. "

Ladies called to ask me, to make my sister Dianne leave her alone and tell stop getting in her business. I said Okay. I told my mother to tell her. Mom said it depends on what mood she is in.

Dianne likes to call to the radio station every day to share information with the city. She says it her way of letting people to know what intelligence going on in the world. One day a lady called to complain about the high water bill. Dianne called behind her and told her name and made some comments. The lady felt so ashamed. She said if I wanted my name on the radio I would have told the audience myself.

My sister Dianne and Aunt Florence were two women that like to visit. They call a funeral and weddings a social event. Wedding can be a topic for weeks. If something happens in Selma they would know within an hour. We had a murder at the movies and Dianne was on the TV with the man wife crying. They never found out why or who did it? My grandmother Lucy said Florence and Dianne are like two dress tails hitting together. They like to stay in the streets. They would start after school then at 6:00 hit happy hour and stay out until 10:00 or later.

I called to talk to Stephanie but Jada picked up the telephone. I asked "where is your mother Jada". Jada said "don't ask for my mother Aunt Janice let me speak to Grandmother Amanda". Jada is 4 years old calls Great Grand Mother Mrs. Jones. I said Jada I need to speak to your mother. No Jada said I want to talk to Matese. I said I will let you talk and pass the phone to my mother Amanda and put my daughter on the phone but ask them to see if Jada will let me speak to her mother. Jada said " Auntie Janice if you ask for my mother one more time I will call the police on you. Grand mother Amanda said on the extension "And the police will come to your house". Jada said "I will tell them they are at the wrong house". Matese gave me back the phone and said I am scared of her mommy. I said. " I 'm not so Jada put your mother Stephanie on the phone.. Finally I got a chance to speak to Stephanie and said your daughter is something else she takes after you mother Dianne".

A man worked out of town as a brick layer. He came in town because rain had shut down the job.
When he got home he showered and decided to go play pool at the local pool room. He said hey to his friends and told them how rain shut down the job and he was looking for his wife. Since I'm here I can take her out tonight. A man spoke up and said well it is just 2:00 she is over to the motel. You can catch her later. The working man could not get what the man said out of his mind because it sounded so matter of fact. So he went to the motel and caught her coming out with her friend. Selma will get in your business, A few months later they were divorce.

Two buses full of mostly men pulled off to Fort. Stewart, Georgia. It was a sad day for Selma the guard. The men had been gone about a week when I saw a fellow's wife left behind. She said our husbands have a few hours off. Would you like to get together and drive up to see the men. I said isn't that and 8 hour trip. Yes 4 going and 4 coming back. I don't know if I love my husband that much. 8 hours and 3 screaming kids (her one and my two). Later both our husbands came home after three weeks. Every thing was in order I love to see him even if it was a surprise my husband. When her husband got home he got a surprised she with someone else. They got divorce soon after.

Dianne told my children they were blessed to come out of their mama. They come from the house of plenty. They throw away too much food. She is always eating at my house while she tells them that story. I tell them that she can not remember half of what she says, yet she here at my house. She complains about my cooking. One day the family was getting ready for a pot luck gathering. That is where everyone brings a dish. She chooses macaroni and cheese. She cooked it at my house and carried to Auntie Florence's house. The roasting pan was full, and a lot was left over. She started putting the macaroni and cheese into containers and looked at me and said "Janice I am fixing this for your children". I said "No thank you they are not use to eating so well they are only use to the little cooking I can do" I refused to take any home, other refused as well.

Janice

While when a person enter a doctor office in a wheel chair they assume
The person is the one to see the doctor. I go with my child, or husband and or mother. I am not the one always sick.

Aunt Mary entered the kitchen where Aunt Louise and Aunt Violet were arguing. Aunt Mary said I am not going to have you two arguing over my mother. Violet, take her out side and get her. They both headed for the front door. Louise went out first and Violet was close behind. They were out side and Violet turned to close the door. She turned around to get Louise and all she saw was wind. She walked back into the house and Aunt Mary asked did you get her? Violet said "all I did was close the door and she took off running, I didn't see her feet hit the ground. She just took off".

My son John with nine of his friend had a graduation party. WE mothers paid $100 each and invited guess to congratulate the young men. The mother got pictures of their babies to young men and posted them around the room. After graduation the party was on until. We mothers agreed it was best to have one party with no alcohol than have them (young men) going from party to party with alcohol. One mother presented her son with scissor to cut the strings.

Dianne got her breast reduce because she was wear in 42DD. After she got out the hospital, she flashed every body with the results. All

the children, adults and any body that asked to see. It did not matter if you want to see them or not she showed them.
I stated having pain in my breast. I went to my doctor and he said it will be better to have them smaller. So I went to the same doctor that Dianne used. He asked me" how small do you want your breasts?" I said "I will like to use a band aid as a bra."

After my son's birth (dry labor) I went to my doctor and ask "what's out now. I do not want any more children". He said "you can get your tubes tied, cut, or burn". I told him "to tie them then clip them and then burn them. If I ever get pregnant again I will sue you to pay for its up keep". The doctor said" Don't worry."

I was shopping for my cousin a T-shirt. My mother Amanda was going with me. In her 80's, I gave her a shopping basket and told her I will be right back. I took 5 minutes and was back in the store. I looked around the store to see where my mother would be. The clerk said do you want me to page her. I said no let me look in the bath room. I did not fine her. I said paged her while I still looked for her. After about 30 minutes I paged her again. Finally I saw her looking on a rack of sale clothes. I approached her and said "where have you been?" She said "I went to another store to buy a top". I said this is a department store with the basket that is supposed to stay in this store. She said "if they wanted it I would let them have it and come back to the store". I said "Mom why would you leave this store". If you wanted me so bad why didn't you page me" she said. I said "I paged you twice". A lady shopper said "well she could not hear in the other store". I was so dumb founded. I said "you are lucky you are not one of my children because you would get a spanking". A (white) lady listening said" my daughter does me the same way, like she is my mother". I was out number by old bittys, so I shut up and became Thankful that nothing went wrong.

I was shopping in another city when I saw a great buy. Sheets, so I started looking for a set. My aunt Mary started looking too. She had picked a white set. So I asked her "what you are doing". She said "I am picking out you a set of sheets". I said "are you coming over" (to sleep with me and Larry)?

I had Matese in the hospital and came home. My grandparents decided to visit. All I wanted to do was take care of the new addition and sleep. My mother was out of town because her husband Mr. Jones had a brain stroke. He was in the hospital in Birmingham for treatments. He never regained concision, and died on his birthday about 5 months later. His daughters called and said her telephone bill was 400.00. My mother said uhm....
So his daughter got Mr. Jones to sigh (x) a piece of paper to give his check to his children. They didn't tell my mother. It was a weekly check he gets from his job. My mom missed the check and called the job and they said the children said this is what our father wanted and my mom said ok. My mother paid for funeral after insurance. His children wanted their dad burial next to their mother. Mother said Yes that will be fine. Now they refer to her as their mother. She says I treat people the way I want to be treated.

After Matese birth the hospital was giving car seats for free. I am handicapped but I walk with a cane. I had my cousin Renee who is 15 to carry my baby. We walk in and I asked the lady behind the desk for information. She started talking and talking about the program. We would need the signature of the mother and we will give you the car seat. I said okay, where I sign. The lady said I want the mother looking at Renee. I said I am the mother of the baby. My cousin is only 16; we don't have childern that early in our family.

It was raining and I need to go to buy diapers for my son who was 16 months. My daughter Matese wanted to go to the store. I said okay but it will be fast. It had stop raining when we got to the store. Matese did not have on her shoes so I told her to stay in the car because I was wearing my limbs and could not carry her. I got my keys and headed in the store. I was in line when a person said a Volvo just hit a car outside. I said can't be mine I have my keys (shaking the keys) in my

My Wheelchair View

hand. When I got outside I found my Volvo involve in a car accident. Matese put the car out of gearshift and decided to leave me. I did not know that some cars move without the key.

I went out to the car the husband of the lady was so nice. He said their have been accidents like this before and everyone was alright so just let the insurance take care of things. I gave him the information and thought this is a long day. Well when his wife saw her car she cried and turned red as if I slapped her and called the police. The policeman came took all the information and said who was driving and I open the back door and said My 4 year old daughter Matese. She was rolled into a ball crying and scarred.

The policeman looked a scarred and crying little girl and said Matese you drive like your daddy. I went home and waited for my husband. We talked first before he hugged her. We decided to sit her down. We said Matese they don't let little girls drive and don't do it again. She said okay. A friend of the family told mother Amanda that I saw your granddaughter driving in the parking lot. She was doing real well too until she hit that car.

I let a lady hold Matese when she was 2 months old. Next day my baby had bumps all over her face. I didn't know what to do so I call the pediatrician and ask could I bring her in. The reception said we are closing now call back tomorrow. I said I can be their before 12 noon. She said do you want me to put you down for tomorrow. I said only if can't find no one else. I call another place and they said come on in. I called back to the pediatrician office and said take me off your book I found some one who will be her doctor from now on. Matese turn out to be allergy to her make up. I stop letting people hold her.

When Matese was about one year old, my husband wanted another child. I was talking in the grocery store to a lady saying. Yes, people want to know when I going to have my next baby. But when I am pulling my hair out and scramming and hollowing then they will say wonder why, did she had that second kid.

I met a lady that asked me if she should have more children. She had

2 and her husband wanted more. I told her that if her hands are full with the children she got now, think, then tell him you want to get them out of diapers before getting more.

I saw her a month later she said He is cured I said what happen. My husband is off worked on Saturday. I got up and left the house at 6:00 am before any one was up. I went to my mother and instructed her not to tell where I was. The toddle woke him up and the baby next. Before 8:00 am he had called my mother 5 times. I showed up after 8 hour shift.

I gave him all day with his children. He decided to listen to reason.

I have a cousin name Darryl who was in the navy. He moved back home. He announced that our children were soft and he was going to pick on them until they get better able to take care of themselves. Our children would run because he would follow them and hit them. I overheard them talking. I told Darryl to let them alone now. I have never seen all six children unite for one purpose that is to beat the heck out of you. The boys would hold him down while the girls would hit.

Another cousin is a truck driver by trade but have no sense of direction. We were at a family funeral in Birmingham the church was 23rd Street Baptist church on the 23rd Street. We followed to the grave yard and he could not fine his way back to the church and drove 90 miles home.

I went to see my father in law for the last time in the hospital. He had cancer of the tongue and was in the finial stage. I was told he may not know me but I wanted to go. My husband rolled me in my wheel chair into the room. He said every time you see me I'm in the hospital. I said you know I can't get up all those steps (12) at your house. He said I could have built you an elevator. I said now you tell me. He said I was not a good father-in-law to you. And I was not a good grandfather to the children. I told him "That all right it will be all right. You don't have to worry about that now. I was blessed with my children and love them because they are wonderful kids.

He talked about some other things with his son. We got ready to leave. And he said I love you both. I looked back to see who was in his bed. I just didn't think it was him. It was the first time he had ever said it to us in 20 years.

After my father in law died a lady called me and said he didn't like you. I told her I know but I think he had a different view what a handicapped person can do. I could never fit that mold. I break any mold set and make my own.

I joined a mother's group called Jack and Jill of America. Each mother is responsible for an activity per month. This October was at one mother's house. She went all out with decoration with the theme Halloween. They dress in costumes and even told ghost stories. She had one room closed off. She gave a warning to anyone who enter into this room it can be hazardous to your health She got her flashlight and ask who wanted to be first to take the tour. Not one child took her hand. She said I don't believe this. She started calling different one's name to come. My daughter Matese said I don't pay people to scar me. I can do that my self. My mother taught me that. She asked again and no one did. So...... .She put the light on and said come on in. The children were amazed to see the decoration. She had gone and gotten the theater department to help. They had a coffin, snakes, rats, skull you name it. While the children were looking around the room going ooh and ahh the lady's daughter sat up in the coffin. The mothers started peeking in the door. The hostess started walking back toward the entrance and turn off the light. The children started running. I was at the door looking in when they started to push. I said just let me get out of your way. Give me a minute. The child said "TOO LATE" pushed pass me. The pushed knock me down flat.

Larry and I were walking with this couple to an event just chatting when I ask her what size she was. She said size 8. I asked this lady how she keeps her weight down to a size 8. She said she only eat one meal a day, breakfast in the middle of the day that is all. I looked at my husband and said you don't deserve a woman that thin.

My Brothers

When we were small my brother Willie would tell us stories. All the cousins were in a back room of the house, and he would tell us bloody bone. We were scared, and then he would get up and announce "I am going to get some water". All of us say "are you coming back?" he just laughs and says "of course".
Willie left the room, (where there are 8 children under the age of 10 years old) walks out side to the window and knock and say I'm bloody bone.
We all ran.

Willie was playful but fair. One day he gave all his possession away. At 16 you don't have much but records, little things. We asked how come? He said he had a heart attack. My sister said No you must have had heartburn. He took everything back.

Cleophus age 18 was a foot soldier of the Civil Right Movement in Selma. He said one day he and his friends Terry Shaw and Charles Bonner, were following Dr. Martin Luther King and were being chased. The car rolled over 2 or 3 times down gully and landed on the tires and they kept going. They were tear- gassed many times. He marched until he got drafted.
Nolen was marching and my mom had told him not to march one school day. Mom being a teacher was scarred for the children and of losing her job. The Dallas County superintend called her at school. He told her, Cleophus her son was in jail for marching. When he did not say you are fired.

Mom would go to the place where they were holding the marchers and pick up not only her son but their friends. She sometime made two trips because it was so many Marchers (children).
My mom told Nolen 16, to go to school not march. Nolen went marching. Next day mom was listening to the radio the announcer said if you were marching on yesterday, go to the church Tabernacle Baptist Church. Mom said Nolen, go to church not school, for further direction. They made that announce on the radio.
Nolen had a hard time with the police, they harsh him almost every time he got behind the wheel of the car. Nolen left town before, he finish high school. And most of his friends move away right after they finish high school.

My mother in law gave me a baby shower for my first child. We are at my mother in law house. We did games and open present. When my brother Willie turn to me and said "Janice Don't fill the house up with a lot of babies". I looked at him and said, "I live in my own house don't you fill the house you rent from me with a lot of babies. He bought the house.

My mother went to a cow farm to get manure to put around her flowers to make them grow. My brother was to help and I was along for the ride. They parked in the pasture and got out a shovel. It soon was boring just sitting in the car so I though I would help by pointing out the big dumps to pick up. My brother got upset and said if you don't stop I will put the next pile in your mouth, I said "Mom did you hear what he said". My mom was tried of the both of us joking around said "Yes I heard him and you better do 1 or 2 things, 1. Close you mouth or 2. Roll up the window." I was shock.

We were watching television when Willie wanted some water and said so many times. Togo his nephew 2and half years old left the room and came back with a cup of water. Willie said "Thank you Togo," I said "Willie where did Togo get that water before you drink it. Togo 2 years old is only so high, he can not reach the sink in the kitchen, or the face bowl in the bathroom, now think before you drink?" He took the water to the kitchen and got his own water.

Willie announces he was going on a diet because he was 15 and was getting in the school band. We were watching television when he made his pledge to loss 10 pounds. Mother looked at him and said" Little Willie you don't want to lose too much weight because you have a big head.

My brother Nolen was 15 and had a learner permit (license). He wanted to go some place and asked mother could he use the car she said no. He went to ask Willie Hobbs his father who lived with Mozell. Daddy said yes and let him borrow the car. We were looking out the window when we see Nolen driving the car in the front yard, then the police right behind him. He got out and the police asked to see his license. He said I have a learner permit and showed it to him. The police carried him down to police head quarters. My daddy went down to head quarters and picked up his car.

Nolen had a little daughter name Aisha 2 who cried when her daddy go out the door. She would cry crocodile tears and say "I want my daddy, I want my daddy". My mother said "you want me to put him in your pocket". She said "Yes". So I had a little talk with her. I asked her" if she like to eat or wear pretty dress and bread". She said "Yes". Then let your daddy go get them for you, when he is out of your sight he is working to get those things for you. Days later she would hold the door open for him to go out, and tell him bye, with no tears. Aisha now had daddy in her pocket (picture).

I have 3 cousins (Bernard, Baptese and Roslyn) around the same age. I had Matese when I was 28. I was the first in this group to have a baby.
My cousin Bernard came over to give me a break. My daughter was 16 months old and very active. I had just been food shopping and was putting the food away. When Bernard walked in and said take a break

I will see after Matese. I am going to read to her. I said just let me finish putting the food away. No he said go take a break. I said ok and rolled in my wheel chair to my room. 10 minutes later I could not close my eyes. I got up and roll back in to the den and found Bernard sleep in a comfortable chair. Where was Matese? I found Matese sitting on my kitchen table throwing eggs on the floor. I got Matese and rolled my chair to Bernard and woke him up and told him to go home.

Nolen got married to Linda while I was in Penn. They had 2 children 14 months apart. He divorced Linda and had wanted to get along. Nolen got the children and brought them to Alabama. His family could help take care of 2 toddles which is a real job. In later years she decided to get them back.
I saw her on the Phil Donahue Show talking about how she had a baby by a priest. One person asked did she (Linda) have other children. She said No comment. I called my brother and told him I taped Phil's show will send him the tape and to get ready because she will be after us next.
Sure enough she did. She through she could get what she like because mothers have rights. My brother had a secret weapon. He had a letter written by Linda saying he better come and get his children or she would put them up for adoption. We don't do that in our family.
They met for a hearing in Atlanta, Ga. And judge said let them stay with their dad. And Aisha and Hasan can visit and their birth mother will have to pay their way back to Georgia. The children were 15 and 16. They met at the airport and Linda pass them off to an auntie. Nolen said "oh no we need names numbers and where they will be at all times". The children stayed for 2 weeks ad had over 50 calls from the family. We have a big family. They got alone with every body but you guess it their birth mother. In time they have grown to except her and even understand her.

One day my brother (12th grade in 1967) and his friends decided to throw a party. They talked for weeks about the big day. He had his sisters, help to get things ready. The mood had to be just right and the lights. The drinks and food must be finger sandwiches easy to eat. The big night came he had to pick every body up (in the one car). The girls were cheerleaders and majorettes for fun, fun, fun. The guys got drunk and had to go home first. The sisters had to keep the girls company between trips every body was home before 10:00pm.

I had been in the hospital for a long time and when home my brother Willie wanted me to make pork chops I said I forgot how to make them. He said just wash them and bake. Okay I put them on and went to bed with all the medicines I had to take. Two hours later I asked "how did they taste". He said what? The pork chops. We went to investigate and found them burnt.

We were headed to church and saw a car that looked like my brother's car. I said to my mother "that could not be Willie's car because the grill in front was broken". When we got home we found Willie skinning a deer. I asked his new wife "What happen?" She said I was coming home when a deer jumped out and I hit it. Some cars stopped and asked if I was alright. I said, "Yes now help me get this deer in the trunk of the car". I came home and told my husband as he was walking around the car what happen and open the trunk so he could see the deer. He said "My wife knows what to do, hit a deer bring it home it becomes dinner."

Willie Jr. got all his friends to give blood to his sister because she was in a car accident. When Janice finally, came home to say thank them all for being so generous by giving blood. Janice told them she feels like a beer every now and then. All his friends drink. That made their day.

Robert was a little bit drunk when he came over our house with his new pet. He said he found it and it took a liking to him and it was his friend. He came to see Willie but Willie was not at home. Robert decided to wait for him. Robert sat in a chair with a squirrel running around his head. He closed his eyes and this squirrel was running all around his upper body. We woke him up and told him that Willie will get in touch with him as soon as possible and he can show his special friend if he's still around. He said the squirrel could do tricks. I didn't want to see.

Willie and his friends play in a band. The band was known as Gene and the Dynamics. My cousin Jackie called them Gene and Goddamns. Willie played the trumpet, Robert played trumpet and so did Charles. Sax-phone was played by Larry, trombone by Chuck, and Gene played the guitar. They played on week ends for extra money. It gave my brother and his friends a touch of independents where they earn their pocket money.

My brother Nolen remembers the day he saw daddy running from lighting. In 1962 the neighborhood we moved into had out house (bathroom outside). Willie Sr. was in the out house and a storm came up suddenly and all you could hear was a galloping horse through the house seeking a safe place to hide
Nolen and his wife Brenda were at a McDonalds ordering food. He said he wanted a salad and his wife order a hamburger. While she was eating he told her the story about McDonald using kangaroo meat. Nolen hopped up and down the food area until she finished.

Willie had a friend from Africa. He decided to change his name to an African name. He and his friend called this name one week end while visiting from college. He went to A&M University in Huntsville, Alabama. I did not understand why Willie wanted to change his name to something that sounded like Whoobe Shoe. Well if that was not the name we called him that name until he said he change his mind.

My brother and his friends earned extra money on the week end by doing odd jobs. This week end they were painting a house. Next door lived some girls. The girls were sitting on the pouch from time to time. Willie and his friends want to get their attention. Well finally they did get to talk. The older one said you are ugly. Willie said no see I am dirty in my work clothes and I can go clean up at home shower and put my good clothes on then………you will still be ugly! The girl said. His friends laugh.

My Husband and kids

I met my husband in a club where I was working. He was a friend of the bouncer Fred. Fred introduced us. He asked me for a date. We went to the movies to see I can't recall what. Larry was late so I thought. I went by my cousin's house and he agreed to go to the movies with me. When we arrive Larry was there and we saw the movie. We carried my cousin home. We went to a different club for a drink. We wanted to be left alone to get to know one another. We talked and made dates in the future. Whoopi Goldberg Show on Broadway says it best in one of her show; talks about a handicapped girl getting married.

I was cooking when my new husband walked in. Looking into the pan and said "my mom cooks salmon with meal and turn it this way". I cooked salmon with flour like flat jacks. I said you miss your mommy cooking, go over to her house. But if you want to eat then eat whatever's here!

Before we got married a lady told Larry, if he mistreats Janice I will hurt you I will get you. Larry said "You will have to get in line because a lot of people told me that. She thought for a minute and said "I think I will jump in front of some body just to spit on you, because that line will take to long.

Larry and I were in the library in Birmingham, Alabama looking up his great grand father patents. It was a learning experience that his great grandfather Joash Sturther, had a total of 6 that started in 1906-1930 and used his ideas on cars and lawn mowers. He knew Henry

Ford but did not receive the money Henry Ford. The Sturther's family said they wanted him to be recognized for his work. After Joash's death his wife sold and burned the rest of his ideas.

Larry is a fun loving and will to give his last to help anyone.
Larry is accident prone he had the strangest things to happen to him. A rat bit him because it was stuck in a washer he was cleaning. He killed it and took it to the vet to see if it had rabies. It did not. He dropped a car batter on his foot. He got a nail in his foot and hit his hand with a hammer. I call him a walking disaster. He broken his arm and it took 6 to 8 weeks to heal. He has had over 15 operations: on his back, neck, shoulder, and knee. Hand, elbow, he had an operation one morning and his father died 10 o'clock the same night.
Larry had an Uncle Buster whose name was Craig Cephus, whom lived in Mountville near Tuscaloosa. One day his Uncle wanted to get a hornet's nest down. He got all the things and started toward the nest. He tripped and the jar with the gasoline hit the nest. And they got behind his uncle. The Uncle went running around the house four times with the hornets close behind. When I .... Get around .... Next time...Open the door.

We decided to go to Lamaze class before our first baby. It had been 10 year since I had time taking care or being around with babies, so I used it as a refresher course. The instructor was a mother of 2 that also was a nurse. She had six weeks to get us ready for our bugle of joy. There were 6 couples which happen to be married. Two couples were black and four couples were white all first time parents. Our instructor gave us exercise to do. She would say Mrs. Town get in a position that won't harm or will not hurt.
Our instructor showed us a film to let us get a chance to see what labor may look like. The film showed a lady raking leaves getting pain and checking her watch. Go into the house to make sandwiches for her husband. Telephone her husband to meet her at the hospital. Then she has the baby with a smile on her face. The instructor, after the end of the film asked if there are any questions. I raised my hand. She

said "Yes Mrs. Towns." I said "I have change my mind I don't think I want this baby," I continued "I can't do what we see in that film". The instructor said "I think it's too late". The class laughed.

My son got in the car from baseball practice, and said "my coach doesn't know what he's doing". I said "what are you complaining about? The mothers pay for the party. The mothers pay for the trophies. The mothers have to get you to all the practices and games, now what are you complaining about. I should be the one complaining".

My doctor asked me how much medicine I wanted for pain when I had my baby. I told him "to wake me up the next day, she has already been named. I want no pain". We went out to dinner. A lady asked me, when are you having your baby? I said today, but since it's a no show I decided to go out to eat. Next morning I was in labor. My husband carried me to the hospital, after a couple hours they wanted to send me home. My husband said please keep her. My mother gave birth in a cab in New York. So just call my wife's doctor and keep her. I got an epidural and went to sleep. When labor pain got intense I found my husband sleeping in the corner of my room. Only a lady in labor knows what was going on in my mind. He was looking so peaceful. In the labor room was my husband telling me to push. The doctor told me by listened to the heart beat the baby was a boy. He was in place to catch the baby. I said doc what is it? He said "I don't know but it just bites me." I said it will be able to take care of itself". Then the doc said, " Mrs. Towns we were wrong. You were right having a girl". That's what I knew in my heart I had.

Larry called the Lamaze class and told them I had the baby. She was just one pretty girl. He told them I didn't make him a sandwich to eat. I told them on the extension that if I made him a sandwich he could not eat it in front of me. Larry fell asleep on the chair in my hospital room. He's lucky I didn't throw something. They asked about Pain, Knowing they had to go into labor I told them not too bad just remember it dose not feel the same going in coming out. Two weeks later we carried Matese Amanda to visit the last class. Larry talked again about a sandwich and how I didn't make him one.

One night we were in bed, when the children asked for countless glasses of water. I told them to go to bed, but we want a story the children said. No go to sleep. A light came on in the bathroom, so my husband said, "Who ever in that bathroom is going to get a spanking!" Total silent then an answer came back, "I'll spank you back!" My husband didn't say a word because it was my mother's voice.

I heard something out side and wanted my husband to go and investigate what's the noise. My husband said," If it's out side leave it there". I said "what if it comes inside then what"? Larry said "then it will get you first because your side of the bed and I will call the police".

A classmate mother pass, I carried food for the family. My husband and I attended the funeral. On our way home my husband say "What's for dinner". I said "Hamburger helper". He said "what did you carry the family". I answered "chicken from Kentucky Fried." My husband said "wait just damn minute you mean to tell me you cook hamburger helper for us and carried Kentucky Fried chicken for them I am going with the chicken".

Lunch hour was over and when I got home I found my mother with a broom handle guarding her room. I asked, " What's the matter? Mother said," I saw a snake!" I said, "Where ?" Mother said," Coming down the hall". I called my husband Larry on the telephone. Larry will you find it and kill it. Larry came home to help. Larry looked and just about to give up when mother said "I see it behind you" so Larry jumped in a turn around way and found the baby snake hiding in a dresser drawer. It was no bigger than a pencil. Larry talking to the snake saying "don't be scared little fellow I am not going to let them hurt you." Larry took the snake to Wallace Community College.

Our son wanted daddy to investigate what was scaring him in his room. Larry closed the door; talking loud telling whatever to get out and stay out. Open the door and told our son it was gone. Larry then, acting as if something or someone had tugged him back into the room. Larry looked around and John was gone. Mommy something got daddy in my room. I look up to see my husband laughing and said "Bill Cosby did it". "Not to his real children "I said.

To get him to sleep in his room again, I gave him some monster spray. I would get my perfume ($ 50 an ounce) and spray his room lightly. One day I could smell my perfume strong through out the house. I investigate and found John spraying his room, under the bed, hall way, and the bathrooms. I said "What is up with that?" John said the monsters are coming out during the day. I said (crying) you must have gotten them. My full bottle was now empty.

I got my husband to spend time with his daughter. He decided to take my advice and take the 5 year old roll skating at the local roll skate ring. When Saturday came they had a date. He got busy and couldn't take Matese to skate so I decided to take her myself. She went around once then on the second turn she fell down. She did not move. I walked over to her and asked what wrong dear? She said I am waiting for my dad to pick me up. I said WHAT? She said "when I skate and fall down my dad always picks me up". I made her get up and carry the skates back to the counter and went home.

John was 4, sitting at the kitchen table, when Matese says," there's a girl name Kitty barrowing me at school". John (pre K) said "I will come around the corner to your classroom and take care of her. … Wait a minute how big is this girl, how old is this girl?" She is about my age 7 and about my size, Matese says. John said" Then you will need to take care her yourself".

When John was in Kindergarten he met his teacher and her assistant. On parent night I got a chance to meet them. I spoke to the assistant first Ms. Patsy. I asked " If your name is Patsy why does John call you Ms Pepsi". Oh you must be John's mother? Yes I am. Well I introduced my self to the class and John is the only one calls me Ms. Pepsi, which is my first name. "What is your name: I said. She said " My name is Patsy Helewski, I didn't know what he would come up with knowing the whole name". When I got home I told him that I met Mrs. Pasty Helewski not Ms. Pepsi. I worked with him to call her Mrs. Helewski.

Mrs. Walker called to speak to my 5 year old son and asked a few question? I wanted to know what is going on. On the phone she said her son came home with a big knot on his head and said the teacher did it. The next day Mrs. Walker was at the school to talk to the principal and the teacher. That teacher flat out denied the incident happen. So the mother said I talked to my son and one other student and John Towns. The teacher looked at the principal and said I am sorry for any miss understanding and apologized. Mrs. Walker took her child to another school.

I always spent one lunch day with my children at school in a month. That way you can be on top of school work and whatever else (behavior) come up. It was a boy that came and sat by me said "Mrs. Towns I try to be good but I hit John and he will hit me back. I said Carmichael maybe you should just not hit him. He said "I will try". The funniest things happen at that time.
One (white) girl would ask me (every time) if I was John's only mother? I told her "Yes, the only one I know."

After my son was born I receive a birth certificate in the mail about a month later. On the certificate the mother's name was Hall not Hobbs. I refused to keep up with it so I called the agent that work in the office in Montgomery to see what I will have to do to change it. The lady I talked to said I should not do any thing to change the birth certificate because it is not that important. I said what do you mean it is not important? I am his mother and I don't want my name wrong on my child birth certificate. And if it's not important, then why do they ask for the mother maiden name.

The zoo trip was a day, two adult (handicapped woman) with four children, (two 10 years old and two 8 years old) going to visit animals. We saw monkeys, elephants, snakes, birds. Some animals were inside and some outside. The gorilla was inside. We enter as some visitors were exiting. Three boys (Hasan 10, Togo 10and Larry son Larry Jr. 8) and girl (Aisha) were taken turns pushing my wheelchair. Larry was excited to see one gorilla pregnant looking mean. One big gorilla was in the cage by himself. My boyfriend Larry decided to play with this gorilla. He made hand gestures, first a wave. Thumb up, point, pate the top of his head, whatever gestures you can do with hands. The gorilla did it all and with each gesture the excited gorilla would wait for the next gesture. The children were laughing. On the top of the cage was a sign that read "PLEASE BE CONCIDERATE DON'T KNOCK ON GLASS"
Larry had made all the gesture he could think of when he scratch his head. We heard a big knock, knock, knock. The gorilla did the knocking, that place clear out so fast all but me in a wheelchair. Larry must have gone 10 yards then turned and asked the four children behind him where is Janice? I was in my wheelchair with all their drinks all over me. Larry peeped around the entrance to see if I was alright. I asked them" What is so funny". I had on white pants with red and orange drinks in my lap. The children laugh to this day.

When Aisha was 12, I asked her to get my pocket book out the car. It was night time and she wanted an excuse not to do it. She said "I can't go because Freddie cougar and Jason were out there." I said, " You think characters from the movies will be at my house. Freddie and Jason will not go any where unless they get paid. I have not paid them so chances are they won't be out our door". I pointed "Now go get it."

Togo, Hasan, and Aisha cornered me before I got married to find out how my marriage will affect them? I told them they are not my children. You are my sister and brother children, you all will go home with your parents. You can come for the summer or Christmas vacation and I will be glad to see you.

Aisha was in the sixth grade when she decided she was not going to school. I asked why? She said "There are aliens in that school and they don't like me". I said, "I don't care if they are aliens, as long as you are back before 3:00 when I pick you up to come home ".

Hasan told me he has fits. Aunt Jan did you hear me I said I have fits. I looked at him and said really. Then he said "Do you want to see?" I said Hasan, you want to know something I have fits too. If you show me yours, I will wait until you finish then I will pitch a fits to put you to shame.
He didn't show me his fit and I did not show him mine.

I baby sat for a cousin, Gwen's son T.J. was 2 and tall for his age. I though this could be fun. I have a king size bed, I put him on one side to go to sleep. Well one hour later the boy kicks in his sleep. Another hour later he kicks again. This time I move to the foot of the bed. He found me and kicked again. I moved to the head of the bed again he found me and kicked me. So I left and got into another bed. Next morning I went back into the room to find him on the bed sheet on the floor. Now that is where I should have put him in the first place. When I took him home my cousin Gwen said "did I tell you he kicks.

My cousin is a hard sleeper." I am having a baby and I know it's hard to wake me up" she said. I told her not to worry children have a way to get sleepy mothers up. Months later she told me. She was sound asleep and she woke up to an empty bottle hitting her in the head.

Sandra my cousin was in Love with a boy named Frencie. I wrote a poem

That's Love
Frenchie and Sandra was sweetheart.
At least that's the way the story goes
Frenchie bump her arm while she had a comb in her ear
She couldn't hear for a month
She got a knife at him because cooking
He was mad about something She drop the knife
He needed 9 stitches to close the wound
He wanted to know why she didn't come to the hospital
They always fight about stuff that seen silly
They had fights over her sister house
And gave the sister a black eye.
Sandra asked what would I give her if she married him
I told her the batter women shelter number.
They had a child instead.
I told her a good lover doesn't make a good dad.

Sandra's niece got pregnant at 16 and her sister Joyce called and said she was disappointed and upset and cried. Sandra said you have a daughter 23 two sons 21 and 18, you are lucky pregnant has not happened before now. Sandra went to her 18 year old daughter and told her to take the birth control pills or she will super glue the patch on her arm. We don't want any baby here.

I attended a funeral for a six month fetus. Joyce's daughter was upset when she went in to labor and the fetus died. I don't know what the normal is but they had programs, 3 preachers, and a soloist. The family arrived with the casket in the mothers lap. After the service the older sister, open the casket and arrange the clothes as if the fetus like it was a doll. I got gone.
Telephone ring and the other end hanged up. Not once but several times. I asked who could do this. Cousin Silvia said it (her brother) Bug's girlfriend calling to fine him. At my house Bug lives next door. She calls and asks for me and got mad because I don't know where he is? We went to a shower for a family member. This girl came with

Bug. I rolled (in my wheel chair) over to the table with a smile and I said, "Sweetie doesn't call my house any more. Every time Bug leaves his house, he dose not come to mine (next door) so don't, call my house looking for him". Later I heard she told her mother I jump on her. The mother said there are mean girls in wheelchair.

Sandra wrote a check to a lawyer and the check bounced. She asked her mother for the money. Then her mother came to my house where convene I was getting ready for a trip. Sandra need 300 will repay in two weeks. Aunt Florence said she will pay the cost to send it. Two weeks later Sandra sent 220 and a note that said it will be another two weeks for $80.

Dating

Dating is a lot of fun but not for me, it was hard. One reason I could not run.
I dated this boy friend that met me in November wanted to marry me in March. No sex or nothing but we only met since November. So I said no. November we met and had a few dates. December we went to a club and he showed a little jealousy. I told him that I am a bi-level amputee that gets around with a cane or walker, or a wheel chair. Who can be jealous of that and live with it? January he wanted me to met his family. I said no! So he told me he would shoot and kill my sister (Dianne) so I said okay go ahead. He said if he would shoot her, well I felt she could run.
He called and told me he was out side my door waiting for me at all times of day or night now they call it staking. When he couldn't put a scar into me, he told me he was on drugs (pills) and wanted me to feel sorry for him. I couldn't, we broke up after that. Years later his wife shot and killed him.

I talked to a guy at the club where I worked as a ticket clerk. He told me he was married. I felt he would bring his wife and let me meet her everything was on the up and up. One day his lady call my house and told my mother she found my number in her husband's pocket. Then she went on to tell my mother how her husband disrespects her. Letting his women friends come over to her house and she had to run one out. My mother said I know my daughter was not at your house but you won't have to worry about her any more. Now I tell you what

tell your husband to stop disrespecting you. That man was so shame. He never spoke to me again.
From that moment on I didn't give my number out to any one. I made them give me their telephone numbers.

A girl saw her boyfriend with another girl. She went home so he could not see her. I said I know she is not in my family. I would get a table then walk over to their table and say. Hope you are enjoying the show. Put my finger in his face and say don't bring your ass over to my house again. Now have a nice time. It is *good* to see you.

I was talking to an ex boyfriend, telling him why he was my ex. He lived in another city and didn't write or call. He was back to attended school for college. The summer was just about over. When I got a call from a girl, she said she was going with my current boyfriend and what am I going to do about it? Children planks can be mean but they can backfire. I just listen for a while when I heard laughter in the back. Then she hung up. The next five minutes a call came my boyfriend who asked how were I doing. I do not lie. I told him fine but I just got a call from a girl who did not tell me her name. She said you are her boyfriend and what will I do about it? My ex is here and we are discussing it at this time. I hung up. He called me three times that night to explain and ask for forgiveness and please don't break-up with him.

My Uncle Bro had been married for over 40 years. When his wife died a number of ladies wanted to talk to him and feed him. One lady made a trip to meet his family in Alabama. She seen to think she had made plans of marriage to him and he would just go alone with them. I asked Uncle Bro if this lady had an inside track to his heart. My Uncle Bro said, " I have been told where to put my shoes for over 40 years. Now I can put them any place I like. So no I think I will just keep my shoes (with a wink)

A senior football player called and invited me (10th grade) to go out. I asked where? He said a party on Union Street. I said I will have to ask my mother? He called back and asked if I was ready. (I never asked my mother because my mother raised 3 boys). I asked again "Where"? He said you are with me and that should be enough. I told him my mother wanted the address and the phone number where the party is going to be. He never called again.

My cousin said her friend, said she thinks its best to marry an ugly guy because then that is love and you won't have woman trying to take him. I told her" No, don't marry a man that you can't stand to look at. If you can't look at him don't bring him my way. You have to be able to see him in every light and midnight. If he scars you?, don't even think about it.

My aunt Elizabeth said not to marry any one from Selma because everyone are cousins. I married a man from New York my cousin married a man from California so we listen. One boy cousin married a girl from South Carolina. None of the cousin married any one around our church.

I decided to go to Teddy Pendergrass concert. He was going to be in Birmingham about 95 miles away. The bouncer's wife also wanted to go.
So I said, "She can go with my cousins and me". Fred and Ruthie has always been a couple. They had 2 children and been married a long time. The night of the show, we had to leave 3 hours before time because the drive was 2 hours and other traffic. We were at our seat when Teddy invited 15,000 women over to his place. Ruthie said "Janice just tells Fred, Teddy Pendergrass invited me back to his place. And that is what I'll be." I looked at her and smile then I said "Ruthie I will whip Teddy Pendergrass ass because Fred weighs close to 300 pound all muscle. YOU are going home". When we returned home Fred cut on the pouch light. "You think Fred wouldn't mind huh?" I said

My Wheelchair View

Ruthie called to tell me I could have Fred. I told her, He was my husband's best man at our wedding. But Fred told me a long time ago, when we worked together, he did not eat leftovers. And if you are at my house, Fred (You) will eat leftovers or you will be left back or left out, and cook for yourself. Ruthie cooks a fresh meal everyday you better keep him.
Sandra was in my car when she saw her boyfriend in the car of another woman. She orders me to follow them. It is a good thing I am driving my car. I said " No I will not. What you can do is talk to him when you see him".

A lady had three daughters. She says her girls sometimes give her a hard time at night before they go to sleep. Innless Cups of water, trips to bathroom. Want to read a story. Her husband don't have those problem all he has to do is clear his throat and they are asleep.

I was in the hair dresser and a lady was at the shampoo bowl. She asked for her purse. Then she announces she was hungry. The attended came in with a drink and said your companion got you this drink and said you owe him a dollar. The lady said, "Tell him I got alligator money while he has lizard money. I asked "what is that?" She said I have that grip money. Then
She pulls out peppermints and asks if I wanted one? I said I have never heard that turned before but I will not for get it. After she explains I said about the peppermint…No ma'am.

I dated a guy, for a one or two dates, it did not work out.
I had not heard from him for months. Then out of the blue I got a call from jail. He called me to bring him fruit and candy. I told him no. Then he said did I know any one who will bring it to him. He said he was in jail for breaking a window and not having the money to pay to have it fix.

The girl scouts take a trip to the next state for fun. Selling all those cookies

Janice Hobbs Towns

Can be hard work and they look forward to the trips. This year we were on our way to Georgia: Six flags and a water park and the Martin Luther King Center. The children were excited and this year we could get more mothers involved to go. I though this should be fun because in the past only two mothers had to take care of 12 girls and about 5 tag along. The girl scouts leader used the same drivers for every trip. The bus drivers are in his 70's and his back up driver was 70 which he kept calling young man. We had 12 girls and this year we had 7 mothers. My friend Linda and I been on every trip with the girls. All we did was line up the girls for event after event. No question just line up.

Three mothers in back did not say much at all.

Two mothers complained every step of the way. The weather was cold for their children. One even made the statement that she was only there because of her daughter several times, until I told her I was there because I wanted every one of the girls to have a good time and go back home to their mothers safely. She stopped saying it around me.

We went to the hotel and the two ladies decided to order pizza and took the orders of all of us (which is about 10) it took from 6:00 o'clock to bring them back at 10:00. We felt so hungry for hours that maybe we should have them delivery. They had to go to a sandwich shop down the street to get a salad. That is what took so long, it was okay we had to wait.

Six flags were fine. The next day we could not go to the King Center because those 2 mothers did not get their children up on time. They miss the continental breakfast and couldn't get the bus packed in time. The bus driver got tried of them, and told me so.

The girls told their leader too many mother came on their trip.

And it is safe to say I will not go with those two women again any where.

Rev. Tuck was the choir director and had practice that began at 6:00am. My daughter told Rev. Tuck that she loved him but the practiced early in the morning has got to stop. They had practices after school until 6:00pm.

My Wheelchair View

The Selma High Choir takes trips on their spring break. Since both of my children were in the choir I decided to go to. The tour started in Jackson, Mississippi with a concert 2 hours long. After eating at the local restaurant, McDonald and Church's chicken. We were off with the two buses and my van on the highway to our next stop in New Orleans, La. We stayed in New Orleans for two events and ate at the church with the family of the Selma High principal. He introduced his family and taught the children to eat crawl fish and they sang for their dinner. The next stop was Houston Texas at two in the morning. On Sunday the children had 4 events. Church service at 8:00are, a different church service at 11:00am. Then we found out that the one church for 2:00 was on the other side of town (Hour away) could not be because they had a concert at 4:00 at another church. The next day we could go to the mall and stay until 5:00 then go to Atlanta, Georgia. I don't care how you look at it Houston to Atlanta on a bus just sound crazy. Well in Georgia we had a concert. Then we had our last event in Tuscaloosa Alabama. I never felt more handicapped than being on that trip with the children. We had to make sure that the rooms were big enough to accommodate my char
It is safe to say I will never go on any more trips with that choir.

One trip to Florida changed our lives. Aunt Florence and Uncle Albert (Dough) were going on vacation with their 3 children, Joyce, Sandra, and Albert II (Bug) and two nieces Baptese and Elaine. The nieces need an overnight bag. When they came to my house to get the bag I wanted to go. I begged my aunt to take me. Eight people were in a yellow Volkswagen. Uncle Dough was driving his wife in front seat, five of us in the back seat. Bug was in the little compartment at the back window or his mother's lap this is before baby car seats. On our way we saw a man hitch hiking. Uncle Dough said buddy all you can do is point the way, we are all ready full. We laugh and laugh a since of fun was in the air. We left at 5:00 in the morning to go to the beach in Florida (where? Who cared)? We stop for breakfast at a restaurant, to order what we wanted to eat. Uncle Dough was known to be a penny pitcher. We did not want to be told you order too much when we were just guess so all the nieces order the same thing grits, eggs, toast, and bacon. His daughters on the other hand order egg benedict and French toast. His wife order just coffee, and Bug order was for free because he was under 2 years old. Uncle Dough ordered a big breakfast because he was a big man 6'and 200 pounds. The nieces ate their food. Joyce and Sandra didn't like the way their food look or taste. They wanted to share the nieces' food, we said NO you order you eat it. When it was clear they were not going to eat their food, Uncle Dough said "Wrap it up they will eat it later." We made it to the beach and had a good time. In and out the water, up and down the beach, while Uncle Dough slept in the car. All of a sudden one person spotted Uncle Dough walking on the pier. We ran to met him. We caught him just before he took a dive in the water. Uncle Dough hit that water and all we could hear was "Shit! Shit! Shit! This water is cold. Shit! This water is salty. We laugh. We all dive into the water behind him laughing. Swam to the beach and sat down. Hour later Uncle Dough announced we are on our way home.

Joyce a cousin of mine came by my house and picked me up. She wanted me to listen to a lawyer explain a situation to me. I listen to his words carefully He said " I have been retained by you cousin to write a letter to get her baby back from her sister in law. The lawyer have written one letter and she gave me a check for 100.00 and now I am getting ready to write another letter for her to return the child to your cousin the baby's mother. Both look at me to see what I would say. I said I have 2 questions: 1) Do you have Alabama and Georgia license. He said "No!" 2) You say you wrote a letter to her husband's sister to bring Joyce's baby home. Let's just say you write 2 or 3 letters and you get no answer what then? Well I don't know. I looked at Joyce and then the lawyer? Well, why am I here? Joyce said to pay the lawyer money to write the second letter. I said "Joyce don't you know how to write a letter." The lawyer put us out his office and town up her check and said he will not take the case and send the second letter.
In my car I said "tell me what is going on?" She said "Mark (her husband) wanted his sister to raise her baby girl, because she had too

many children to take care of. He feels his older sister that lived in Georgia and wanted a child. He was willing to give her his baby." He told Joyce you can see her whenever she wanted. On one trip to see the baby his sister said the baby is sleeping and no you can't see her. Joyce said "I am her mother you mean to tell me I can't see my own child this is a 3 hour trip."
So Joyce wanted her baby back. I said that is easy called the police and say, this is my baby birth certificate and this woman have my baby pick it up please unless you sign something. I sign a paper giving her the baby to help me. But I went to a family gathering and everybody ask to see the baby and I could not explain why my sister in law had my child. I will get you in touch with a lawyer in Georgia because my brother is going through a hearing with his children. And don't you sign anything but Mickey Mouse on the dotted line from now on. Don't say nothing to Mark it will be taken care of. But I don't have any money" she said. I said "Joyce it will be taken care of". The cost was…. Priceless.
AT the hearing they got their baby back.
Joyce named all their children after her husband. She divorced him after he stabbed her in the face.

We decided to take a road trip with my mother in law to New Orleans. She had a workshop for her job. On the way we had a lot of laughs. When my
Husband, Larry stopped for gasoline; his mother asked me "What will you do if Larry cheats on you? I was caught off guard. I said oh I have never had a problem like that. I guess I will have a strong talk with him. Later….. I told Larry what his mother said but this time I gave him this answer "You know I took a gun course and can't shoot straight. You better not find out what I will do. I can make your life a living hell after all I have my sister Dianne". I gave mother and son something to talk about.

I had my second child a month early which means he had some problems. He was in the incubator. My son was pre-term 6lbs 2oz and 20inches long at 8 months. I was in an unsure mind because I didn't know what to do next. My father in law came into my hospital room and said "Now you have a girl and boy. You don't need any more children. I was shock then said Thanks. Then he left, I wonder if it was that nice or not. I wanted to know, who (Died) and made him boss. I wondered who told him how many children he could have. It took two weeks before my son was well enough to come home.

My cousin called me in the hospital after I had my second child and asked where he was? I told her in the incubator because he is a month early. She told me months later that I shocked her with my answer. I always told her she could not count because she had her 3 children 3 week early every time. She wanted to tell me who miss counted now. When I told her he was incubator and they would not let me hold him. It knocked the wind out of her sail.

We were at my father in law house for dinner. When he began to begged his daughter to have a grand baby for him, in front of me. My father in law said "Please, Please, have me a grand baby daughter". She said "No not until my husband finish medical school". Her husband did finish school and had his practice. Father in law got sick and died. His daughter said the only thing I regret is not having a grand baby for her dad.

We travel to Arizona to visit Larry's uncle John and Aunt Mable. Uncle John took us shopping. After looking around everyone got hungry. When we got to the food court, everyone went in different directions, I seen to be at a hotdog shop. I asked the clerk to show me what he sells. I saw pinky, regular, large ex-large hotdogs. My husband and aunt came back at the same time. What do are you doing? I said this man is showing me the different size of his winners. The man turns 2 shades of red. We got pizza.

Uncle John was a window shopper. He pushed me down the hall ways. I will be in my wheel chair and he would see a loud color with poke

-a-dot and say that will look good on you. I would say no but I know it will look good on you maybe on your head. We laugh and look for more outrageous thing to talk about.

My brother died June 4, 2005. We were in Mobile for a nephew wedding. The rehearsed/dinner the night before was rocky to say the least, and seen to be a little strain. We were in the hotel getting ready for an active day. The day of the wedding we were looking to see family from Atlanta, Montgomery and Selma. My husband told me the wedding has been call off. I wanted to know why? We finish breakfast and still not talk to the groom. His children decided to go swimming. I said give the children a break, while they swam we adults can sort out this mess. I told them not to go without and adult or someone older to watch. Matese said she will go because she has taking a life saving class because she was a girl scout. Cinque went down and did not come to the top of the water. My son John drove in and saved him. Togo told us that the wedding was call off because, her mother had invite more people and wanted him to pay the different in coast. He felt the fiancé should speak up and say mom "Lets, just do this" She didn't he got mad and she called the wedding off. Then we got the call from Selma my brother was found died in his house. I called back to Selma and told them don't come. I called the Atlanta group on the cell phone told them to turn around. The wedding is off. My niece (traveling from Atlanta) said we are half way there and I said turn around and go home. I will talk to you later. I got to catch the Montgomery group. I didn't catch them, but left a message. I told my nephew I had put out for 2 tuxedos and 2 rooms for 2 nights. I drove to Mobile (3hours) turn the wrong way on a one way street in front of a cop (policeman). You are not getting married.
Well now if you plan a wedding on a hill top in your sock and drawers' don't call me.

Janice Hobbs Towns

I wrote two poems for my niece:

Little Foxy Lady by Janice H. Towns

Little foxy lady is no mystery to me
She was a happy baby
When work is done from 9 to 5
She will now come alive
With a new husband by her side

We love her and want the very best
Which makes no difference to the rest
It will put Charles Vashon to the test
To prove to all they won't take no mess
When Aisha made her choice
We all came together with one voice
That is to say; Much Joy, Best wishes
And Happiness for years to come

I asked some of my friends "What does marriage really means"
By Janice H. Towns
God keep Him first and always
Love, Honor, Cherish
Surrender your share of the covers
Give up the remote control of the TV
Look for lost items (remote, keys)
Get ready for some awful smells
Cook for
Pick up after
Check behind
Let the seat down or wipe it up
Yelling your name from every corner of the house
For the rest of your life

My Wheelchair View

Matese Towns age 12 Selma, Alabama

Mother
My mother is a very sweet person, someone that cares
She is a very neat person, someone that is there
She is the one I tell my secrets to
The one who holds me through sad-times
The one who tells me what to do
And help me control my mad-times

Her hope is as big and strong as a mountain
Her love is more powerful than a tide or a fountain
Her courage is stronger than any on earth
Yet all of these things have no worth
She tells me great stories of long ago

She tells me things I do not know
She can walk into your heart without any feet
And she has powerful speech
I'm crazy about my mother
And she is crazy about me too
If she dies, I would not know what to do
My mother's heart is as pure as gold
A smile that sparkles like silver
And a spirit like flower that never withers
She may be as old as sand
But she is my Best Friend

My daughter made this poem for me. I loved it so much.

Things people say:

I was in the store when a lady decided to tell me how I had gain weigh. She began saying," It's only been almost 2 years since your wedding, you have gain so much weigh". I said I'm pregnant.

A man came by our house to say I didn't look bad. But before you were in a car accident you looked a lot better. I had only been home a week.

Sell clerk came over and asked "make I help you" me in my wheel chair. I said I am looking for a blouse. The clerk came back with a blouse and asked my sister if I would like it. Ask her (in the wheel chair) if she like it. The clerk refuses to acknowledge me.

My husband had guard duty for their 2 weeks training in Mississippi. A lady said "It is a shame your cousin spent so much money in her wedding and her husband has left her already within almost a year". I told my cousin to tell her, "My husband Larry must not know it because he had to come and pick up supplies for the Guard Unit and slip by to see his wife".

When I became pregnant my mother's friend would call every day to tell me
A story or other people bad pregnant stories and out comes.

My stepfather died this lady Ruth called to tell me how she hated that man. I told her don't worry yourself about it. He felt the same way about you.

My Wheelchair View

A lady, whom had a stork, was in the hospital sitting at a table. When one of her friends came up and said, "at least you are not in as bad shape as that girl" pointing to me. I was in a car accident I did not have a stork. Some people don't know what to say.

Mrs. Smith was called by a lady that said I just saw your husband with another woman in his car. So Mrs. Smith told her "not to worry him will get around to you if you just close your mouth. You can be next. I am Mrs. Smith and I will remain Mrs. Smith until the end."

I went to Steak Pit to eat lunch with a cousin. A lady asked me my name I told her and she told the person she was having lunch with my whole life story. She told of my mother, father. The accident, my cousin died in the accident what kin she was to me. When I got home, I told my mother about that lady and told my mother" you better be glad it the same story you told me".

Mother and I were in the grocery store shopping. A guy came by several times as if he wanted to say something. When we made it to the check out line he finally made his move. He said "hay you will you give me your telephone number? With out missing a beat I said, "No my husband and 10 children won't let me". He said without missing a beat, my wife and 15 children would not like it too. My mother said if you have10 and he have 15 that makes 25 children in all both should never say a word to each other.

A lady called me from her cell phone and said "You better pick up your children. I see them playing on the street without an adult paying attention". I didn't know who was calling but my children were over to my sister Dianne house. I got over there as fast as I can and picked them up.

I drop off two boys 4 years old at the YMCA for swimming lessons. My sister Dianne was to pick them up. Lessons are half an hour long. One hour later I got a call from Dianne asking me if I picked up the

Janice Hobbs Towns

children. "No" I said "you promise to pick them up". Then she said I'll call you back. Two hours went by I called where are they. I said I will just come on over. I got a call back and she said well we got them now and they will be getting spanked. What Happen well. The two boys saw a cab and got into the cab. Told the cab to turn this way, he didn't see his mom car (because his father was in the car to pick them up.) so he told the cab driver to go up a street and turn at his great auntie house. When they got out the cab they said thank you and auntie forgot to call.

A man called me and said his daughter was in a car accident. He wanted me to give him money to get to the hospital in Birmingham. He told me his wife was ready gone. He needed money for gas and need it as soon as possible. Then he called me by another name (Juanita). I call Juanita and ask did she know this person. She told me not to give him a dime because he doesn't even have a family. When he showed up at my house I gave him $10. Juanita called back and said did you give him money because he lies. He will use it for drugs. I told Juanita he came to my door not hers and no, I did not give him much but at least he left my house. Hopefully that will be the last I would hear from him.

A lady sent her children to her mother for a week. She missed her children so she decided to call and check up on them. It had only been two days. The children said mama you need to come and get us. Grandmother said she is tried of us, sick and tired of us. The lady said she was there the next day to pick her children up.

A lady told me that my family takes advantage of me. My sister and brother had children and I kept them. 3 children under 3 years old, I said okay because I was the best choice to keep them at the time even if I was only 19. We had fun time together as a family reading cooking sleeping and tell stories. The last laugh was on her because those children are successful now. One is a Doctor, another is bank officer, and last one business buyer.

My Wheelchair View

My son was an eight month baby pre-turn weighted 6 pounds 2 oz 20 in long. A lady wanted to know why I had my baby early. She called me and wanted to know it I heard that she was going with my husband, because it was a lie. So I told her NO, that if she would keep that lie on her side of town where she lives

A lady called me and asked if I called her daughter? I said "No". She said I talked to the person myself and she said Janice Hobbs was her name. I said No there are two things wrong with what you are saying 1. I don't know your number (you always call me). 2. I don't know your daughter never met her.

Granddad Frank was in the hospital. He came home to fine out his daughter Little Lucy had gone to the same hospital and family members didn't tell him. He sat down all day in his pajamas. I was 14 at the time and would walk to the hospital to see her. One day out of the blue she asked for her father. I told Granddad that Little Lucy wanted to see him. He got dress and got to the hospital. My other aunts were mad and said I should let them handle the matter. I need to stay out of grown people business. My aunt Lucy died less than 2 weeks later.

Linda was walking down the street when out came a man snatched her purse. He ran she ran behind him caught and beat him up. He got mad and called the police on her. The police came to her house and said "This man said you beat him up and had no reason to do so". She told the police the real story. They told him that if Linda wishes to press chargers on him they would have to arrest him. She said no, I won't press charges.

Rita was at Kentucky fried chicken eating with her sons. When she was aware a group of boy looking around, place her purse scarp on her knee. The boys decided to go out the door close by where she was sitting. Grab her purse and ran. Rita have 4 boys ran behind the caught the biggest part of her purse. We wanted to know was she scared. They got the money but I got my credit cards and pictures. We now call her Rambo Rita.

A new guy moved into the neighbor, a girlfriend took him under her wing. She told him what to wear and bought him some pieces. She told him what cologne to wear. She told him to go to the dentist and made an appointment. They dated she told him where to go. She helped him decorate his house.
He said he had to go out of town. She went to the store and past by his house. He was on a date with someone else. She went home then made a trip to his house. She didn't say anything. She went into the house and pick up some things put them in the front yard and lit a match. He called the police. The police listen to his side of the story. Then she said " I helped this man get out of a shell. He told me he would be out of town. I saw him with a new girlfriend, so I felt he did not need my help any longer. I picked up the things I bought and burned them hear are the receipts. The police said well sir we can't really do anything. Its (Clothes) her stuff and she can burn or do anything with things she pays for. After the police left she hit him and told him to call the police now. He said hat is alright.
My mother and I went to the home of a church family member because the mother had died. Three Jones boys married to three sisters. The mother of the boys died. She died after being in a nursing home for a number of years. The father of the girls died and hour after the lady died. My mother and I decided to pay visit with 2 cakes and drinks. My mother is a generous person, gave the boys and their wives $50 each. She also gave the mother of the girls fifty. One day after the funeral a sister of the girls called and said she wanted a token too, and will be over to pick it up. She came by and my mother gave her a token.

I talked to a nurse in the hospital, and said are there any mice in the hospital because I am scared of mice. I am glad there are no mice in the hospitals. The nurse said I saw one wheeling in the wheel chair coming down the hall way.

My Wheelchair View

One nurse had three children at a young aged, two girls and a boy. She got a divorce from her husband. Now being a single parent with 3 teenagers (18, 16, and 15) in Birmingham she wanted to keep them safe. Her son 16, had a curfew of 9:00. His younger sister started at every night 8:30 saying "Mama you make him come home to early, He need to stay out until at lest 10:00. Mama the girls don't talk or dance until 10". Her mother says, "Well just as long as he is back before 9. I have to go to work and don't want to worry. It is the house rules". They go back and forth and then the door bell rings 9:00. She runs to the door, saying proudly "That's my brother".

In the rehab we are to get on your own as soon as possible. If you need assistant in getting to get up Get dress and get going. There was this one lady that stayed in the bed and called the male nurse Johnson over and over again. One day her family came for a visit. Johnson went into the room and said, you didn't call me today. The lady was from another country with broken English said (Johnson) Husband, Husband.

In rehab I met a lady that had 20 night-grown all colors. The grown count 20 to 25 with robe to match and shoes. She love being in the hospital. Mrs. Hightower had an order in which she starts example blue, green, yellow and once she get to the red she goes home.

I was in the Children Hospital with a roommate. My roommate had to go to the hospital next door for some test. On her way back she decided to pull the covers over her head because it was windy. She heard a little boy say mother move the mother say why son. I don't know what's coming but I am getting out of its way.

There were a couple in rehabs that liked each other. He had got paralyzed from a shooting and she had been in a car accident. Some one asked him if he liked her. He said yes, but we can only be friends. Why? He said with both of us in wheel chairs we can't get up to get each other a glass of water.

Janice Hobbs Towns

Juanita is my friend that I met her in rehab. I am a girl that just shows me the way and I can go get it type. Juanita was a caution person mad because she did not listen to her (inter) voice. She got into a shooting accident at a club. I wanted her to write this story because we became friend. I am a bubbling personality enjoy life that talked to the nurse and everybody. They would bring me things cards, food. and little things that make my day. I appreciated everything and would say so. Juanita wanted to be transferred to my room so she could see everything. She found that being mad did nothing. So we would talk and talk about men money the further. After talking so much we cry a while then we would say what can we do about it? Nothing! Then we Laugh and Laugh some more. Then she got out the bed and started joking and playing and talking and having fun. Before long she was just like me. I got my driver license. So I said Juanita, they have a program at Spain Rehab Center to help people in wheel chairs get their license. I said Nita go get your license she said no I don't need them. I said yes, you do too, because when you have your own license you can go where you want to. And not wait for somebody to decide what to do for you. Now I can't keep up with her. She is always on the go.

She has been there for my wedding. She cooked the potato salad for my wedding dinner. She is a wonderful cook the best in town. Most people say so not just me.

She helped me through my pregnant days. Now the babies growing up and she is still very fond of them.

I talk to her every week because she is the one to know what's going on.

We have been friends for 30 years.

After my story was in the Enquire I got a letter from Penn. It was the largest piece mail that had ever come through the post office in Selma. They put it in the paper before delivering it to me.

Marsha was one of the people who wrote to me. She was around my age but lived in North Dakota. She wrote when she got married and when she had her (3) children. She had a girl and two boys. We sent pictures of our family to each other and told stories of what going on in our lives. I wrote her about my boyfriends. When I got my husband and children, we have had a 30 year old writing relation.

She told me about her son. Andy (19) was a red head boy with cute eyes. He meets a girl and loved her. The girl was not saved she was at odd with her family telling him all the details. He did not know how to just listen and not act. He was always trying to fix the cause. Once he has a solution to one set problems, she came up with another set one. You know the kind that always have a game going on. But you don't remember the one start when one end a began. Well, at a party was at a friend house. The broke –up couple meet up there and talked. She told him she wanted to kill her self. So he left the party and parked his truck on the train track. She called her mother because once again he trying to control her. She didn't want to die after all. She had her mother pick her up and take her home.

He stayed on the train track for a while in his seat belt. A (UN) schedule train came through and hit him. That night he died. His friend said they didn't know? They didn't know what this girl was about?

They didn't know what affect the girl had on him?

They didn't know but through someone else would tell his mother.

Marsha said her son was changing but she didn't know why but felt he was just growing up. She didn't know any teen killing themselves over a girl.

But now she knows, we all know.

Her husband went into a deep depression and she could not reach him. He took all the pictures and could not say his son's name in the house. She wrote me and it broke my heart because I have a son. When I got the letter that said she divorcing her husband I wasn't surprised. A death of a child will pull you together or tare apart.

It kept me on my job as a mother just being aware how break up affect our children. Love is good but not a promise but it don't kill. You must move on.

School days

Ms. Murphy asked her class how your mother deals with hard headed children. I want you to tell me some of the thing your mother say.... one boy said my mama says bring you ass here...the children say... ooooh. One girl said, my mommy say bring you butt to me. Last boy said "My mommy said carried your heart to God.... but bring you ass to me."

We had a basketball game in Birmingham in 1970; Tipton High School made it to the play off. On the way home the bus caught fire in Bibb County. The sheriff stopped us and everyone on the bus was a little scared. Your bus is on fire said the officer. We got off running. Everyone but Eloise an eight grader we through was crazy.
Eloise said she would not get off the bus. She said she rather burn with the bus at 2:00 in the morning than go to jail. Centerville gave us one of their school buses to go home, but wanted it back before school started later that morning. The principal came out (of his bed) to see where we were the bus was. He told us that roll will be call at the end of the school day because of all the trouble with the bus. He told the teacher and their children to get in his car to take them home. Mr. Robowski was a hand on principal. The next day back to the play off was announced on the PA system all who wanted to go the bus will leave at 4:00. My mother asked me if I wanted to go back to cheer the team on. I said No I will pass.

A lady (mother) wanted to know why the bus was crowed. She asked the principal of Tyler school in 1962. Rev Dawson said we have asked the superintendent many times and had been given the run around he said he will try and it may take a while.

The lady said I will take care of it. The lady called the superintendent office and asked for a bus for Tyler school. She told him her name and where she lived. The answer, he gave her was the same as what he told the principal. She said we really need a bus. Then he said I have told you my answer, do you want me to call the sheriff. She told him I know his number and if the sheriff comes to my house I will have all my children lined in the windows with rifles in their hands to respond. Now, you don't have to give Tyler a new bus, because Southside (a white school) bus pass by my house and I will put my children on Southside's bus it is not crowed. Next school day, Tyler had a New School Bus.

When I was in the 6th grade, the girls would pick someone to be mad with just children prank. Well today they picked me. They talked about my mama (I didn't have a mother but two bald head papas). I though they may know my mother better than me.

They talked about my dad (I didn't have a daddy I had two bald headed mamas). I would not say a word all day. They walked me home talking the whole way and picked one person to fight. Not like today where a group jump on 1 person, in our day one person picks one fight. So when I got on the pouch I turn to the girls that walked me home and said " Thank You for walking me home. My mama wants to thank them for seeing that her little girl got home safe and sound. She also hopes they make it home safe. We would not want you to get hit by cars. So thanks again, remember I will be here at the same time tomorrow.

My cousin was with that group supplying them with little person family business (That I had bigger bust size than my auntie). I told my grandmother How I suffered that day how Baptese betrayed me. Grand mother whipped her. Baptese told them since none of them got whipped, so if you pick Janice pick me too! Next day they picked someone else.

When I was in the 8th grade a girl name Eloise would say "Who ever took or touch my paper or book, "Your mama ain't got on no draws".

Janice Hobbs Towns

The class laughed. Then one day she got a piece of paper off another girl name Eloise's desk so Eloise Wade said "Whoever got my paper off my desk Your mama ain't got on no draws". Eloise walked over to the girl's (Eloise Wade) desk and pushed to it the floor with her still in the desk. Yelling to the floor in the girl's face and said "My mama got on her draws."

I was a person that hated to fight. One day a girl decided to fright me over her boyfriend? I don't remember why? She said he liked me so I had to fight for him. The thing is I did know him. So I told my mother and my mother walked in before class started and asked for this girl and said, "Why do you want to fight my daughter. My daughter doesn't know any of you this is a new school for her and she is here this summer to get to know a few of you before school starts in the fall. The girl said I don't want to fight your daughter. My mother said "good, now that is settled".

Matese was in the third grade when her teacher was Ms. Taylor. Ms Taylor was a good teacher but she disliked children as a whole. I wanted my 8 years old to have a good experience with no headaches. So I toured after school for one hour. I would go over her work and if any student stayed after school I would help them too. Brandon was one student that had a problem with his teacher not his work. I was going over some work when Brandon said that Ms. Mayfield did not move his seat. She had moved all the other children. He was mad he said He will get a dog teach him to bite Ms. Mayfield. He will get a cat teach him to scratched Ms Mayfield's eyes out. He got snake, turtle, and a rat. I told him, Brandon (You) could go home …..Dismiss.

I worked around the school whatever way I could. The book sale was one of the duties of the mothers. For one week the children could come in and out.
The children would come and pick out a book and the mothers would help them select. Then write a recipe for their purchase so, teachers would know they were not just trying to get out of class. It also let

parents know how much they spent and on what. I was talking to the other mother about how the names had change from Mary, Jane, and Sally. I was writing a recipe for Candice. My daughter's class was in with their selection and they wanted Matese's mom to write their receipt. Roshonda, Rashonda, Brandon then one boy said Ms.Towns I want you to check me out. I said okay what is your name Deramus Hickenbottom. That was my last receipt for today.

When I was, in the 7th grade my book got stolen. After school at the famous Hudson High, I was putting books in and out my locker. When two older boys came up behind me and took one book. They begin throwing it back and forth in the hall. They threw it away and could not fine it.
I started crying and a teacher looked down the hall and called all of us in to his room. I heard the teacher say Son while you do that taking her book where is the book? The boy said I don't know. Well don't do it again. I went home and told my story to my cousin Baptese who told me that the boy was the teacher's blood son. I was so mad. I went to the teacher class room and told him that if I knew the boy was his real son my action would have been different. The book his son got and threw away I will not pay for. No, I never found it but his father did pay for it. I did not.

Caroline Studivant

Amanda Studivant Callen married John Callen
1. Fannie Jones 5 boys
2. Elizabeth Cunningham Bill
3. Louise Young
4. Florence Dukes Thompson
5. Lillie C Cleveland
6. Lucy C Kelly married Frank
7. Charlie married Florence
8. Bud married Bell
9. Creed

Janice Hobbs Towns

Lucy Callen Kelly married to Frank Kelly

Amanda Hobbs Jones
Mary Sewell
Lucy Kelly
James Kelly
Jermiah Kelly
Frank Kelly
Annie Cunningham
Violet Kennon
Florence Hatcher

Lizza and George Tate
Frank
Catherine
Joe
Spook
Rosa
Pearvella

STORY TIME

Uncle Charlie was married to Florence but still like to go out with his buddies. Aunt Florence over heard some talk about them going out. So she dressed in his clothes and started walking down the road. The man in the front of the wagon see her, Lets pick that guy up for a ride, Uncle Charlie recognizes his clothes and said no, no let not because that's my wife.

Aunt Lillie had 12 children by her husband they called Bullet. Bullet like women and one got bold and started talk to my aunt. Finally my aunt told her you need to stop because I am raising a daughter that will take your Husband. Sure enough, Lillie Mae did take that woman husband and had 6 children and stayed together until he died.

Lula Carson was my great grandpa John's sister. He got cold one night and started a fire. The fire got out of hand and burn down the house. Grandpa John died that night. Great aunt Lula had to stay with us until her house got fix. She stayed with us for six months. She was well in her seventy's. She went to the bank to do business and because she refused to put any one on her bank book. When she died her estate went to the state and divided her estate between her nieces and nephews. My grandma Lucy got 63.50 after all fees taxes and law fees.

Aunt Lula went to church down the street from her house. After a sickness, the deacon from the church would come and pick up church dues. He rode a bike, One day he came by and said Sister Carson next

Sunday I will pick you up on my bike you can ride on the handle bars. She just laughed.

One day I ask my grandma Lucy while was she so busy and always have direction for children to do. She said "Oh girl, I can work a half dozen girl at one time". I looked at her and said "YOU HAD A HALF of DOZEN!!" Amanda, Mary, Lucy, Annie, Violet, and Florence. Five teachers and one nurse. All had BS degrees or Masters Degrees and one went on to get a Specialist degree. And three son that got grown and gone.

Uncle Bro lives in New Jersey and I was visiting from Alabama. His wife had some relatives over for a BBQ. My uncle and I were sitting on the steps when we heard his wife, Catharine saying how many places she plan on going to visit. I looked at her husband and said "Uncle Bro are you going to let your wife go all those places." He said "She can go if she has some those died presidents. Died president what does that mean. He said "She would need Franklin, Jackson, Lincoln, and few more of the others because the live one can't do any good.

Alvin Callen Tate was on the birth certificate. It seen Lucy's mother Amanda didn't like the name and said I want this baby named after me. From then on they call her Mandy. After grand mother marry Frank Kelly the name became Mandy Kelly;
When my mother was ready to retired form teaching she had to have her birth certificate in order. She had 2 teachers to write letter saying they only knew her as Little Amanda Kelly.

Frankie was a teen boy from Newark. He came to the south to go to school for one year. My 2 girl cousins and I walked to the store about 3 blocks from our house. While walking we heard a dog barking. We got scared and run to the other side of the street. Frankie got in the middle of the street pulled his belt out of his pants in one tug and told that dog to come on out and get his ass whipped. We waited, and found the dog to be a toy poodle behind a locked screen door. We laughed all the way home.

Frankie had a way of tripping you up and say get up before you fall. He was name after our grandfather Frank. We were going to the church to fix something. My grandfather was always fixing something (light sink bathroom whatever) at church or some sister's house. We got in the car, but no one wanted to sit behind grandfather. Frankie got to that window and claimed that seat. We said ok. Frankie said "It's raining". We laughed. Grandfather Frank spits out the window. That is the reason no one wanted to sit behind him.

Aunt Elizabeth is grand mama Lucy's older sister. When we would go to Birmingham, Alabama, for doctor appointments, we would go by to see her and give her sister Lucy's love and one dollar. At funeral time auntie would come to Selma. John was her nephew and his funeral was at our church. My sister Dianne cried and cried. I looked at her surprised. At the end of the funereal I said "I didn't know you knew John that well". I didn't know him at all but auntie was crying in my ear, and so I cried too.

Grand mother Lucy went to the drug store to get ingredients to an ointment that she makes out of house hold things, camper gun, soda, green alcohol, and some other ingredients. She was at the store to get green alcohol but the man only had white. The store clerk said ma'am that is all we have. She said I need green alcohol. They went back and forward several times. The store clerk was tried and said just wait a minute then he went to the back and got some mint and put in the white alcohol. Here you are ma'am and charge her more for the price because of the mint.

Grand mama Lucy broke her hip and the daughter that is a nurse, returned home to help with her care. She was a good caregiver so my mother the older sister said we must pay this nurse. All the children contribute some money and those who could not pay gave their time (spent the night, cook, or clean the house). They all check with the nurse to see what service she needed or wanted. On her time off she had an old boyfriend and they would go fishing, or a drink.

I went to the hospital to visit a girl around my age, but a little younger. Mary Ann's mother was in the room. We were talking when the girl woke up and her mother told her that Janice is here to see you. She said "Janice, we used to p-a-r-t-y". I looked at her mother which was my mother's first cousin and said "I know she is out of her mind because we never went any where together". She had a sister name Janice, she must have us mix up. I did not go to see her any more, and less than a year she died.

Violet had four sons in Newark, New Jersey. Angelo, her second oldest was at a dance with his boys (cousin) from then north neighborhood. They dance with some girls and was having a good time. Some south neighbor boys got mad because one of the girls was his girlfriend. A fight broke out and the boys ran with south homeboys on their tales. The south homeboys had guns that shoot. Angelo got hit. He was only 18 at the time, after being shot they cut him in the stomach. He died on the way to the hospital. His mother is a nurse but could not help her son she has never got over it.

Uncle James (Bro) sent his wife (auntie Cat) for a week to visit. She had been sick. We had an auntie Cat that loved the family so much she made a trip to Alabama 15 days before she died. We were glad to see her. We had a get together at the church and she hugged everybody and she sang her favorite song. The call came on the twenty of July that she died. Five cars left Selma to go to the funeral. I was at the wait when I asked her son why she didn't look the same. He said "She couldn't paint her own face before died. The funeral people didn't know how to fix her face. We all was crying from time to time her son said " If you all don't stop crying I will slap everybody in here and start from the front". He looked up at the coffin and said maybe I will start in the back". I went to the bathroom and over heard two women talking about the church. The Lady said "which church the funeral going to be. Oh, that one we will be ready for any thing". I had no idea what that mean....

When arrival at the house, to head to the funeral. Nothing out of the ordinary happen. We did see a hit and run on the way. This is Newark, New Jersey. When we got to the church we march in and the family left the front seat vacant (for dead person to view the service). The service had the usual song, bible structure, as I knew her. They were singing when a person in the family said "LOOK" our eyes follow the out pointed hand. There was a man with his head down the pastor and 3 other form a circle around chanting something. My 7 year old son got out of his seat to get a better look but he went up next to the coffin. After about 5 minutes went by when my cousin Baptese push them aside and started CPR on the deacon. We have 7 nurses in the family but only one moved to react. We all didn't know what else to do but stop the funeral. The ambulance could not get into the church because the cars had jammed the street. After the ambulance took the man to the hospital, we got back to the funeral. The pastor announce that we were at a home going for Sister Kelly but didn't want any thing to happen to that deacon(that went into a comma) because he was the chairman of the church board. They announce "That food will be served at the church". No one (from Alabama) return to the church. We got into our cars to go to the graveyard. On our way a police tried to hit us. We had to go through a toll booth and pay. One half of the cars stayed behind the body. The other half got to the graveyard about the same time only because we pass in front of them at a traffic light. We met back to my uncle's house. Those five cars came up at different time to the funeral from Alabama. But at 5:00 that evening we all left New Jersey at the same time in a row.

July 26, 1972 at 3:00 in the evening:
A telephone called for Mrs. Hobbs, Your daughter Janice, has been in an accident in Lancaster, Penn. My name is Doctor Means and I work at the hospital. Your daughter has been burned 80% of her body. Mrs. Hobbs we need your consent to treat her and by the way we have to cut

the left leg right away and maybe the right leg too. Mrs. Hobbs do you hear me, are you there? My mother did not know what to do? Janice was in New Jersey with her oldest son Cleophus. She told the Doctor that's not my daughter because Janice is in New Jersey. The doctor said I will call you back. Mrs. Hobbs got on the phone and called her son, by that time her sister Florence came over. They became a team to piece together what's going on. Cleophus called and said I don't know anything. I will go over to Penn and call you back. The Doctor said "This is your daughter Janice and she is calling for you". The driver of the car is dead, but the little girl is okay.

Cleophus reported back and said yes mama Janice has been in a car accident, Earleen is dead and her baby Sharon is alright. Yes she is calling for you.

The question was how did Alabama family know of the accident and Penn did not. Well Janice was in and out of consensus and told them her mother's telephone. The nurses asked question and Janice would answer. Who's baby? "Not mine" I answered "but where is my cousin the baby's mother".

No one wanted to tell me she died. The next thing I remember was seeing Cleophus at the end of my hospital bed. The next day my mother was by my side. The first order of business was to let me know that Earleen was dead. The second order of business was to see what shape my health. How long the recuperation period. A place for my mom to stay that could put her at the hospital whenever needed.

My mother had no idea how to take care of a sick child. I was in a room that had to have no gemes. Sterile room with weighs on my leg.

I stayed in the hospital for 3 weeks. I met some wonderful people Rev Simmons, Mr. and Mrs. Henderson and countless nurses and doctors.

The Swindlers Club got a flight to take me close to home UAB hospital.

In the Birmingham Hospital I stayed for 5 months. I transfer to Charleston South Carolina I stayed there for 4 and half months.

My day at the hospital in Lancaster was spent medicated. The nurses had to wear protected clothing because the room had to be germs free. There wanted my mother to explain to me my condition and also explain about my cousin death. Something my mother could not bring herself to do. So I told her just ask her to confirm what I wanted to know.

In Birmingham hospital day consist of going to the tank. The tank was an over size bath tub. I would have to get into the tank for one hour then they would pull the bandages off. I was taken to a sterilized room to get more bandages on which would take about 2 hours more. When I got back to my hospital room I would need medication for pain. Then I will be place on what look like an iron board to be turn every two hours. My whole day was not a pretty sight, but one I stayed in for 5 months.

The nurses were nice. I had a few who let you decided. She claimed to be a religious woman and I needed the bed pain. She put me on the bed pain and left. I told my mother that I need to go but the bed pain was not feeling the way it should fit. My mother said do what you got to do. The nurse came back and fused for 20 minutes because she did do what was necessary in the first place. Another one was prejudice she knock over and expensive gift and broke it. Never say she was sorry. I also had people write me and send money one nurse wanted to open my mail. I told my mother that a nurse opened my mail and $10 was in the card. We could not fine the money so after that I did not let the nurses open my mail. I was in Birmingham a long time. I had a tube place down my nose to put food in my stomach. I got to the place that I did not like Jell-O. I should say I got tried of Jell-O we had it twice every day. When I developed bed sores they moved me to another hospital.

When I got to Charleston I was place on an air bed. It looked like a water bed but had air blowing so a patient would not develop bed sores. There were two places that had the air beds that were close to Alabama in the United States, one in Huston, Texas and one in Charleston, South Carolina. I had a tube placed in my nose again until I learn to eat. The nurse was cold. The nurses' station was across from my room. If I call for some one to do something they would say your nurse was not available. So I ask will you tell my nurse they would say no. I wrote my mother and told her the nurses were mean. I had a girl to write this letter for me. My mother sent my sister Dianne to help with my care. Thing change when Dianne got there. Dianne kept them on their toes.

When I got home being a 16 year old in a wheel chair I cried.

Sister, Sister by Aisha J. Hobbs

Sister. Sister why is my head so high?
Because my past I won't deny.
Well…Sister, Sister why do you walk like that beautiful stride?
Because I have strong black pride.
So, why do you talk like that, as if only you know?
Because I know where I've been and where to go!
You ask why walk as if I'm royal, why talk with authority;
I am a leader and this is what I'm destined to be
I come from a rich heritage, one I can't forget-one you need not neglect

Black is the woman I am and achieve to be
Black is inside not just what you see
Black is the earth
Black is the sea
Black is the air
Black is you and me
Black is my skin
Black is my soul
Black is the only thing I know
Now sister, sister why walk with your head hung low and talk as if you don't know
When you have a great black seed you must sow!

My Mother

You can tell how a woman is by what she does. My mother is kind hearted and will give a money to a lost or needed soul. A man was selling a CD and sold it for $6. The CD only had 2 songs.

I was in the hospital in South Caroline when Mother received a phone call from her daughter in law. The daughter in law said that mother didn't know how to act like a grandmother. She had not call to see how her new grandson. You sent no letters or cards? Mother replied well maybe I don't, because I put my daughter in your care and she has had a car accident with burn 80% of her body. This is the 3rd hospital she has been in and we are still adjusting to (new city) Charleston.
I am trying to be a mother. So no, I haven't sent you a card or letter because this happened to us in July and your son was born in late August. I had to go back to work (School teacher). It is now January I haven't had time, but I am trying to help my baby. I go to work all week. The weekend I go to my child to be there to help with her care.

We went to the airport to pick up my brother Nolen. We were running a little bit late so we were moving because the plane had already landed. My mother forgot to close the trunk of the car. The trunk was open and my mother was pushing me in my wheel chair and forgot the curb. She was so upset and thinking someone was breaking into her car. Well I hit the curb and fell and scarped the skin off my right limb or stub, it took 2 months to recover.

Janice Hobbs Towns

My mother was looking for her car when her 8 year old son said mommy I know where your car is? Mom, said where? And take me to it. He took her to Mozell's house. Mommy stood in front of the other woman's house calling for her husband to come out. He would not. She and her son walked back home to fine the car sitting in the yard. They got in to go where they needed to go.

Matese 19, was sitting with a boyfriend kissing. Mother called her granddaughter to her and gave her a packet in her hand and told her to use it if she needed it. Matese looked at the picket and found a condom. Matese came running to fine her mommy and told me what her grandmother did. I asked Matese wonder where 81 years old get a condom. This is a great grand mother with ideals.

My mother and her friends would have benefits programs to help any one in need. They had them at different churches but plan was the same. All family and friends and singing group come and give an A&B selection and put the money on the table. All the money goes to the person in need. Most of the people have an illness, accident, or close to death. I just remember one person died a few days after their program, and then it went toward the funeral.

When my mother was in labor with me (Janice) she went to the hospital. The doctor sent her home after one hour because the labor pain stopped. A week later my mother got in labor again. This time pain was consist, St. Jude nurse was trying to assure her every thing will be alright. The nun/nurse told my mother that it can't hurt that bad. So my mother slapped her and said it feels like that. When the baby final came out the cord was around the baby's neck. She had carried four. She knew that pain is pain.
Janice was her last child.

Mother was in the hospital with her children coming in and out to visit. Janice comes during the day. Dianne would spend the night. One night Dianne told mother she needed to think about coming to her house for a while that is until she feels better. Mother said I need go to the bathroom. When she got back into her bed mother felt something strange. Dianne continued my house is quiet with no children. Mother though she was trying to get her in a back room. Mother started fighting with the control of the bed hitting Dianne several times. Dianne called for backup, the nurses all came and tried to talk and calm her down. Mother said Dianne brought her friends and she had to fright her way out there. Mother said they should know how you all you are treating me in here. They tried her to the bed and called security and when they got there Mother said you are in on it too take them all in away from me. When I got there the next morning she told me about what happen. I asked why you didn't call me (Janice). Mother only act that way with Dianne.

The family gathered for a birthday party. Mother met him at the mall to purchase a gift. Later at a family birthday party Dianne came in talking loud.
Most of us can take her in small doses. Dianne said Aunt Mary I call you and you told me that you did not have time to talk to me. You were busy cooking for your grandson from out of town. You and mama get busy with your men (the boys in the family).
Mother said nothing but after Dianne talking and attacking everybody, mother jump up at her swing. I said Mother, (is 83 years old) and I told her Dianne is 53 and maybe you need to ...mother cut me off and said she should know better. It caught my cousins off guard. They separated them
I took mother home. We had a long day, church 9:30-2:00 and party 4:00-6:30. This story is a reminder that all family members do not need to present. Some need to be sent a piece of cake.

My mother had a cousin visiting from the Mobile. This cousin Mildred was a drinking and fun loving person. I was 8 years old with my back to the door. This cousin said almost falling on me I know you are glad to see me. With my back from the door I said No and push her off me. I know now that maybe I should have looked back before talking but my mother was walking in, the door at that same time. I know now, how not to say thing off the top of my head, or to look around before you get hit.

When Amanda was in school, every one called her Mandy. Her teacher said have your mothers' written your name on a piece of paper. The teacher call up Mandy, reading the paper and said your name is not Mandy but Amanda. She said it sounds so much better. She let no one call her Mandy only Amanda.

Lucy, Elizabeth, and Lilly are sisters that lived to be in their 90's, in their right mind until the end. We had the up most respect for the sisters.
Their mother Amanda told her grand children as long as they had nine wholes pointed to the grown they better do whatever she says do. Another saying she had don't go so shit-in ass frighten.

My mother had a way of saying ain't it awful ain't it awful. So someone was telling mother something and her 5 year son Cleophus said ain't that awful mama ain't that awful. She said yes it sure is.

My brother's girlfriend had his class ring and refused to give it back. He tried and tried to get it back when my mother was passing the room and caught him talking to her on the telephone. He explain the situation to mother and she said give me the phone. My mother got the phone and said, "Young lady you will return my son's class ring or I will send the police after it". She returned the ring the next day. She told him to give it to his mother.

Auntie Florence was at a club talking about her niece Janice had just had a baby girl. How pretty and how happy everyone was that everything turns out okay. My husband came home and said "I should say something to Auntie". "For What" I said. Baby mama drawer, His baby mama's sister happen to be in the club and heard her (Florence). He wanted me to tell my auntie to tone it down and not be so happy. I said let me get this straight you want me to tell my auntie not to be happy and to not say how she feels. He said "Yes". I said," You must be out your mind… No." I continued," Auntie Florence is grown ass woman and can say what ever she wants where ever she wants."

When auntie Florence and Uncle Dough were thinking and talking about divorce. They went to the lawyer office. I talked to him after they came back. He said your auntie is crazy. She thinks she is married to Rockefeller she told that lawyer that she needs 1,000 dollars to run her house and child support. I asked her in his office if she was kin to Rockefeller Family or the Kennedy.

At school auntie Florence was talking small talk and laughing with other teachers when the superintendent came by the room and asked what was going on. My auntie with professional and strait face said we are having a decision about education.

Auntie Florence was the type of person that can ask you 10 questions for information. If you don't want to share information she will ask you 5. She love talking and sharing information about you, herself, and any body else. She was like that neighbor on "Good Times" always giving a kind and funny side of life. Her story has some truth in them.

Janice Hobbs Towns

Florence daughter Sandra had a boyfriend Frencie that love to fight. Sandra called from next door to say Frencie was fighting over at her house. Dianne and I decided to get two canes and go over there and ? ?? When we got there Joyce had a black eye and her boyfriend Mark said he would not get involve. Sandra had bruises on her arm. Frencie was gone. Well they call the police and their mother and told her about it and that we had come over with two canes. Instead of my aunt Florence coming home after work to check on her girls. She went to Frencie's mother house and told on us. She told Frencie's mother that the canes were to beat him up and not to come back to her house to fight. She was drinking beer while she told his mother this story.
When she finally came home and told us what she told his mother. I said why would you rat us out like that, why? He had no business at your house fighting.
Frencie is 6'4" tall and weigh about 190 lbs then, now he just say hi (at a distance) when I see him.

My Wheelchair View

Being handicapped has been a blessing and a curse. You be the judge.

The blessing is when people don't judge but help. I had a lady asked, if she Can help me put my chair in the car.

A lady shook my hand and folded up some money and put it in my hand. I Looked at the money and it was 100 bill.

Some will open doors

Don't ignore the person in chair

Don't feel a person in a chair can't hear

Get embarrass when their children ask question

Seem more embarrass to hear the answer

I had people who will roll their eyes as if I am invisible.

I've been to restaurant where people looked discussed as if I were at their table.

I had children hit me in my back while in a wheel chair or pinch me

I had a child walk over and cut off the scooter I was on

Feels a handicapped person made of money

Give no rest days (this for family members that love to go)

Mean well but put thing out of your reach

Talk at you not to you

Kick my chair or shake their foot near the wheel

Janice Hobbs Towns

I love to travel. With a wheel chair it not as much fun but not impossible. A funeral in Cleveland, Ohio a wedding London, England and a trip to Hawaii for vacation

My uncle died and we drove 13 hours to Cleveland. They had the wait and funeral an hour apart. The wait was 10; 00 TO 11:00 and the FUNERAL were 11:00 all at the same church. I had a nice time because my Aunt Jane was a wonderful hostess.

I got sick at the funeral and couldn't go to the grave yard. I got to hot and the food was too grease that I can eat. A handicapped person has to be very careful with food and handle one's body. I stay home sometime because people just can't see from a handicapped point of view. The ramps location the steps things that make you feel uncomfortable. Since our family is so big I always carry the help I need t o get in and out of places. London is not build for wheel chairs. It is a lovely crowed place and the wedding was fun. A wedding in London takes all 24 hours. Wedding at 12:00 noon you go to a cottage for drink and dinner. After the dinner we play casino gambling with the couple picture on paper money. You get prizes for you wins. Then we dance that take place until 2 am. The next day breakfast with the couple then you can check out and go home. My daughter caught the bouquet and they say they will come to her wedding next. I told them our weddings last 4 hours in America. One man told me in Scotland wedding last 3 days all week ends, Friday to Sunday.

I am encouraging her to elope.

The cake was cut with a sword. It had 3 layers and half is a fruit cake with frosting. I left after the cake was cut I went to the room.

The breakfast was eggs Canadian bacon, hash browns, stewed tomatoes, beans, toast milk juice tea coffee. I asked how often England drinks tea. A cab driver said 5 times a day; Breakfast lunch and dinner at ten in the morning and 4 in the afternoon.

There was one bed and breakfast that was handicapped expectable in London my nephew said they are hard to fine. Jeremy and his mother Janis help us get around London and made it fun. The tours are made for wheel chairs but the rest of London had steps and narrow hall ways. I love all the people; they made me feel a part of the family.

My Wheelchair View

I had planed a trip to Hawaii when my children were small. It is beautiful and expensive a cup of tea and toast is $5.00. We took a plane ride for many hours to get to Hawaii rented a car that we could put a wheel chair in which is a middle size car over there. You better know the difference it could cost you dearly to make changes to what car to drive. The hotel was right across street from the beach. We let the children take surfing lesson and walk to take in the culture. There was always someone selling something every where. My husband knew the area because he had been station there a long time before us. We went site seeing and went to Sam's, yes they have one in Hawaii. The polliasm which is like all the Hawaii culture come together in one place about $100 per person. The boom site of Pearl Harbor and pineapple plant and there are countless things to do in Hawaii. We rode around the island saw school children get out for today. Christmas lights and decoration it was nice.

My son wanted to go to the beach to meet a girl so we went to the mall across the street. This mall is 5 stories high, with 2 or 3 parking levels.

John decided to go to the mall to get us. John saw Wayne Brady in the mall

Well we could not fine him (JOHN) and I was understandable upset. I told my husband to go look for John. And to me that was to slow getting info, so my daughter Matese and I went out looking too. We found my husband Larry in a Jack n the box ordering and eating. I said," why, are you eating at a time like this?" I can't think on an empty stomach" said Larry. I was mad. Larry went to the police and was told they can't do any thing for so many hours but need a picture of our son. When he called to tell me this I image the worst and cried. Three hours later John walks into the room. I was ready to go home. When the hotel offered us a card to come back on a discount (I though yea right, in another 100 years).

The star Forest Whither was at my house. My husband carried him to the airport and asked if he had time to meet his wife. Lucky me I was home.

Larry was working on the set and left for work when my children came running in the house saying that a helicopter was out side. I told them don't worry there are no plane crashes that I know of near here. Then a knock at the door came to a surprise. I went to the door and the helicopter was parked on the highway asking for my husband. I told the director he had already left for the set.
He went back to the helicopter with a thanks and he was gone. The sheriff was holding the cars back until they were up, up and away.

We went to The Club in Birmingham to see Willard Scott. In the middle of his show I got sick and had to go to the restroom. He stopped his routine and asked my husband was he coming back. There were just few black people on the other side of the room. We were the only black couple sitting in our area there I felt bad but when you are sick that can't be fake. The waiters were mostly black and didn't want me to leave so I stayed with the attendant in the restroom until I felt better. The attendant gave me some aspirin.
The O Jay concert where we had backstage passes was the best seat in the house.
My husband and I saw Lena Horn in San Antonia, Texas. The spurs game with the 76's with Dr. J. playing was fun.
Milwaukee Buck game was on T V with Atlanta Hawks did you see my son and me.
The Harlem Globe Trotters were fun to see.
Bill Cosby in Montgomery at Alabama State was funny.
Luther on tour had all his audience to sit down while Sinbad talk from the hip looked at me and said "girls in wheel chair will corner you to talk to men". I wanted him to know I have never had to corner any man to get his attention.

CPSIA information can be obtained at www.ICGtesting.com
Printed in the USA
LVOW081451050613

337129LV00010B/1197/P